SCIENCE 5-14

Pupil's Book

P7

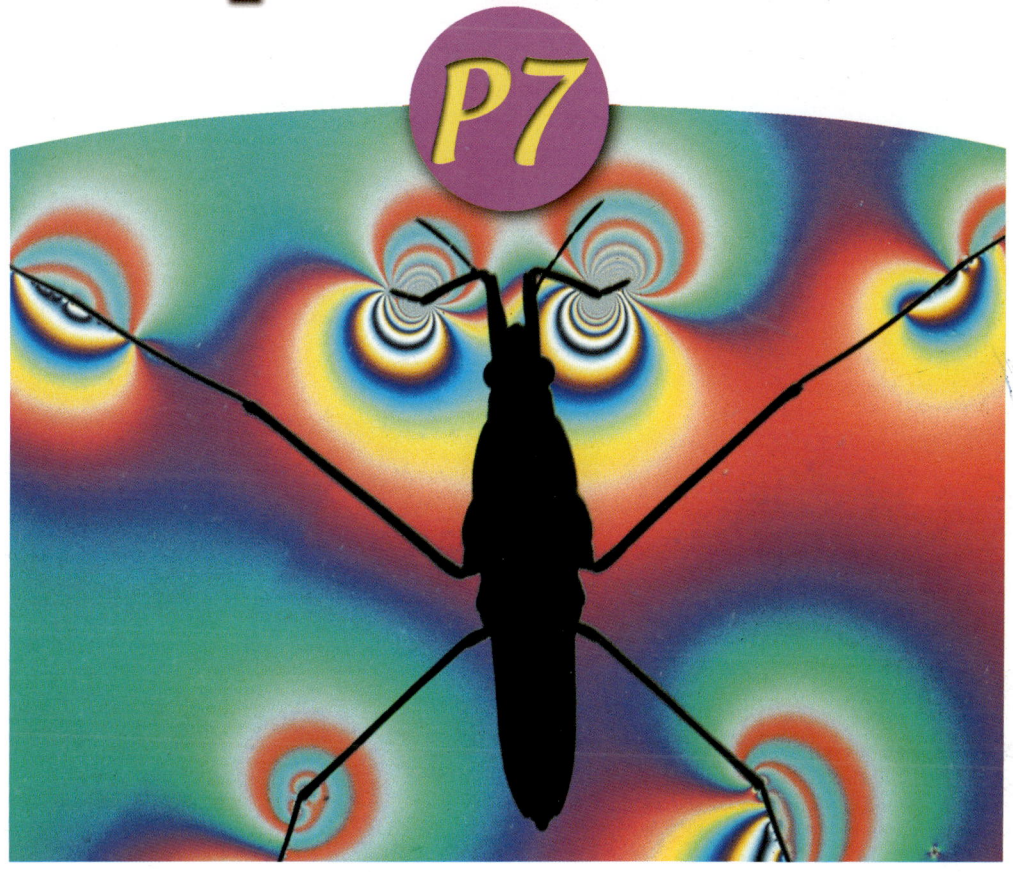

Paul Chambers Jim Marshall
Nicky Souter Rae Stark

Hodder Gibson
2A Christie Street, Paisley, PA1 1NB

Photo Acknowledgements

The publishers would like to thank the following individuals, institutions and companies for permission to reproduce copyright photographs in this book. Every effort has been made to trace and acknowledge ownership of copyright. The publishers will be glad to make suitable arrangements with any copyright holders whom it has not been possible to contact:

Action Plus (25 right, 71 right); Alan Rabinowitz/Wildlife Conservation Society (82 bottom left); Andrew Lambert (63); Associated Press (14); British Oxygen Company (28 left); Bruce Coleman (29 left, 70 (octopus, seal, greyhound, cow, bear, swallow), 71 (shark, gannet, dolphin), 82 (top left), 87, 88 (top left), 110, 112, 114 (top right), 115 (both), 116 left, 118 (frog, habitat), Caithness Glass Ltd 23, Corbis 21, 36 (bottom right, top right), 44 (top left, bottom left), 47 (bottom), 72 (bus, train), 73 (left, top right), 74 (left), 75 (parachutist, top right), 88 (bottom right), 106, 108 (right), 116 (right), 117 (both); Finlay Simon 82 (top right); Geoscience Picture Library (16 left,17 bottom); Hodder (12 (top), 15 (top), 44 (middle bottom left, middle top left, middle bottom right), 46 (bottom left), 50 (left), 51 (left), 51 (right), 72 (all except bus and train); Illustrated London News (27 right); Life file 12 (bottom), 15 (bottom), 17 (middle), (22), 24 (top left, bottom left, top right, bottom right), 25 (left), 33, 46 (top right, bottom right), 47 (top), 50 (right), 52; NASA Dryden Flight Research 75 (bottom right); NHPA/Laurie Campbell 118 (bird); Norman Conquest 27 (left); PA PHOTOS/European Press Agency 73 (bottom right); Robin Silver 113 (both); Sally Anne Thompson Animal Photography 118 (bottom left); Science Photo Library 2, 5, 6 (top right, bottom right), 7 (both), 8 (both), 9, 10 (both), 11 (right), 16 (right), 17 (top), 18, 19 (both), 26 (both), 28 (right), 29 (right), 34, 35, 36 (left), 37, 38, 44 (top right, middle top right, bottom right), 46 (top left, middle left, bottom right), 82 (bottom right), 88 (bottom left, top right), 89, 95, 98 (all), 100 (both), 101, 102 (top right, top left, bottom left), 103, 104 (both), 107, 108 (top left, bottom left), 111, 118 (vegetation, insect); Stock Scotland 109, 114 (bottom left).

Orders: please contact Bookpoint Ltd, 130 Milton Park, Abingdon, Oxon OX14 4SB. Telephone: (44) 01235 827720. Fax: (44) 01235 400454. Lines are open from 9.00 – 6.00, Monday to Saturday, with a 24 hour message answering service. You can also order through our website www.hodderheadline.co.uk.

British Library Cataloguing in Publication Data
A catalogue record for this title is available from the British Library

ISBN 0 340 800410

Published by Hodder Gibson, 2a Christie Street, Paisley PA1 1NB.
Tel: 0141 848 1609; Fax: 0141 889 6315; email: hoddergibson@hodder.co.uk
First Published 2002
Impression number   10 9 8 7 6 5 4 3 2
Year   2007 2006 2005 2004 2003

Copyright © 2002 Paul Chambers, Jim Marshall, Nicky Souter and Rae Stark

Typeset by J&L Composition Ltd, Filey, North Yorkshire.

Printed in Italy for Hodder Gibson, 2a Christie Street, Paisley, PA1 1NB, Scotland, UK

Preface

Science 5–14 has been written to match the science component of the revised Environmental Studies 5–14 National Guidelines. **Pupil's Book P7** is intended to cover content from level C, where it would provide coherence continuity and progression, although the main coverage within this text is towards the targets described in level D.

The book is divided into three sections which correspond to the Knowledge and Understanding outcomes Earth and Space, Energy and Forces and Living Things and the Processes of Life.

As part of the 5–14 programme, pupils are encouraged to develop informed attitudes towards the environment around them. Chapters 19, 39 and 59 allow pupils to develop an understanding of the world in which they live and of current environmental issues.

Science provides a number of contexts for pupils to develop a wide range of skills. Investigating skills are focused on in Chapters 20, 40 and 60.

It is hoped that this book provides opportunities for pupils to relate science to their everyday experiences and that through this process, it stimulates interest and enjoyment in science.

Contents

Earth and Space

Energy and Forces

Living Things and the Processes of Life

1 The Earth and the Solar System

The Earth is one of nine **planets** which orbit around the Sun. The nine planets and the Sun make up our **Solar System**. The Sun is the closest **star** to the Earth.

The Earth is the only planet which is known to have living things on it.

The Earth, like all the other planets, is round. The diameter of the Earth is 12 755 km.

It is the third planet out from the Sun and lies 150 million km away from the Sun. It spins on its own axis and takes 24 hours to complete one **revolution**. We call this one day.

It is moving around the Sun at a speed of 28 km per second. This **orbit** takes 365 days (1 year).

The nine planets which make up the Solar System are arranged like this.

Figure 1 The Earth from Space

Figure 2 The nine planets moving round the sun

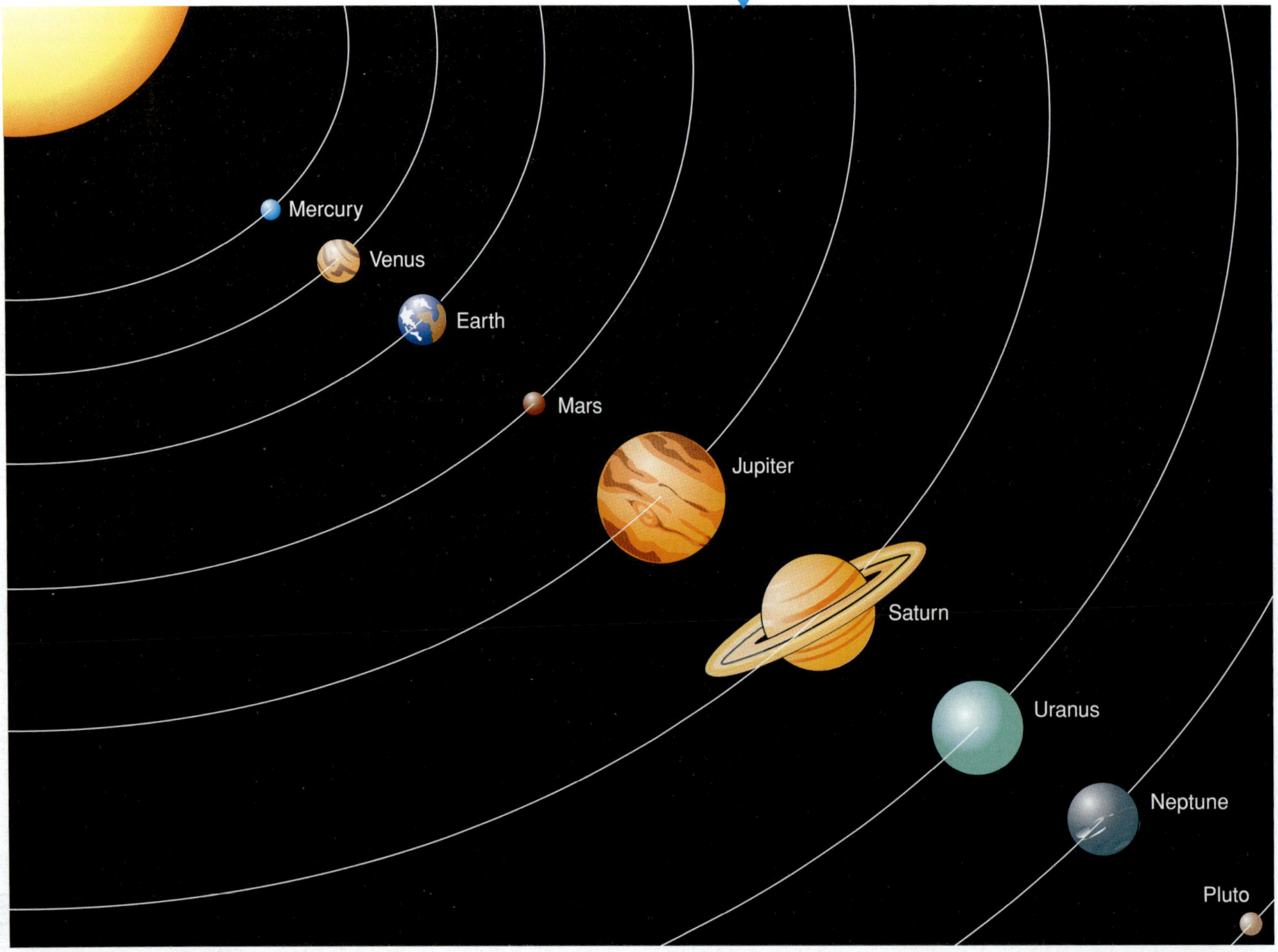

Mercury

Venus

Earth

Mars

Jupiter

Saturn

Uranus

Neptune

Pluto

Each planet is a different size and a different distance away from the Sun. They all spin at different rates and orbit the Sun at their own speed.

The planets are often grouped as the inner planets (Mercury, Venus, Earth and Mars) and the outer planets (Jupiter, Saturn, Uranus, Neptune and Pluto).

Planet	Distance from Sun in kilometres	Diameter in kilometres	Time taken to spin once	Time taken to orbit the Sun
Mercury	58 million	4 900	59 days	88 days
Venus	108 million	12 100	243 days	225 days
Earth	150 million	12 750	24 hours	365 days
Mars	228 million	6 785	25 hours	687 days
Jupiter	778 million	142 800	10 hours	11 years
Saturn	1 427 million	120 500	10 hours	29 years
Uranus	2 871 million	51 100	17 hours	84 years
Neptune	4 418 million	49 500	16 hours	165 years
Pluto	5 906 million	2 300	6 days	248 years

Key ideas

★ The Earth is the third planet of our Solar System

★ There are nine planets which orbit the Sun

★ The Sun is a star

★ Each planet is in a different orbit around the Sun

★ Each planet is a different size and distance from the Sun

Wordbank

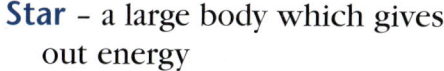

Planet – large body which orbits a star

Star – a large body which gives out energy

Solar System – collection of planets which orbit a star

Orbit – to travel around

Revolution – a complete turn

Questions

1 List the planets of our Solar System in order, starting with the planet nearest the Sun.

Look at the table and answer questions 2–7.

2 Which planet is the largest?

3 Which planet is the smallest?

4 Which planet has the longest day?

5 Which planet is closest to the Sun?

6 Which planet is furthest from the Sun?

7 Which planet takes the longest time to orbit the Sun?

8 Make a bar graph to show the diameter of the planets.

2 Space and gravity

Gravity is a force which attracts objects to each other. Your body produces a small gravitational force which attracts objects around it. However your body is too small to have any noticeable pull.

The bigger the body the greater the gravitational force. Also the closer together the bodies are, the greater the attraction.

Gravity and Earth

Consider the Earth and the Sun. Our Sun is a very large star and has a very large gravitational force attracting the Earth towards it. Therefore the Earth is continually being pulled towards the Sun.

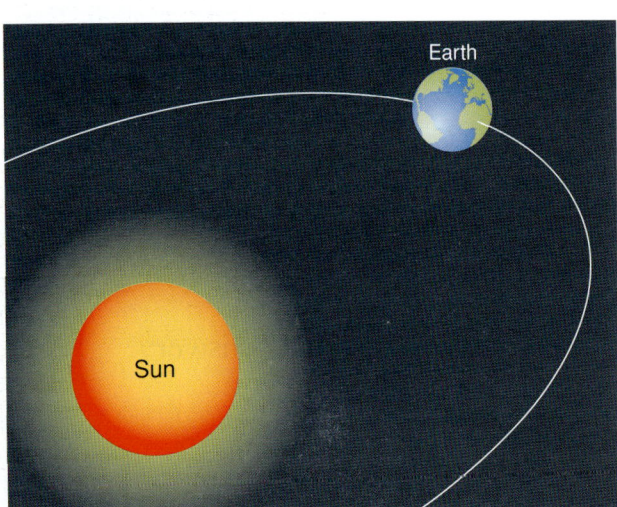

Figure 1 The Earth orbiting the Sun

The Earth orbits the Sun but does not move towards it.

This is due to our planet moving through space at just the right speed so that it spins round the Sun yet does not move closer.

If a boy had a chestnut on an elastic string and he spun it around above his head the chestnut would orbit around his hand. The elastic is pulling the chestnut towards his hand but it does not reach it.

Figure 2 The chestnut orbits the boy's head

Consider what would happen if there was no force of gravity.

If we cut the elastic string then there will be no more force attracting the chestnut to the hand. The chestnut will fly off.

Figure 3 The string is like gravity between the Earth and the Sun

The same pattern applies to all the other planets which orbit the Sun. The Sun's gravity stops the planets from flying off into space because the planets are moving at just the correct speed to stop them getting too close or flying into space.

Gravity and the Moon

Consider the Earth and the Moon. The Earth is the larger body. The Moon is attracted towards the Earth but it spins around the Earth.

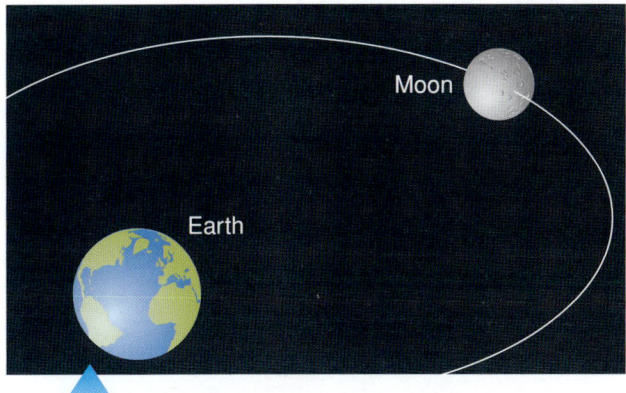

Figure 4 The Moon orbiting the Earth

Now consider a spacecraft orbiting the Earth.

The spacecraft has to have very powerful engines to overcome the force of the Earth's gravity. As it moves further upward away from the Earth the gravitational force becomes less.

The astronauts position the spacecraft so that it is travelling at the correct speed so that it can stay at the same distance from the surface. Once it reaches this correct speed the astronauts turn the engines off. The spacecraft stays at this speed because there is no **friction** to slow it down.

If the spacecraft engines were switched on again then the spacecraft would escape from orbit because it would be going faster.

If the speed of the spacecraft slows down then the gravitational force will cause the spacecraft to come back to Earth.

Figure 5 A satellite orbiting Earth

Key ideas

★ Gravity is a force of attraction between two objects
★ The larger the object the greater the gravitational force
★ The closer together the objects are the greater the attraction

Wordbank

Gravity – force of attraction between two objects
Friction – force which acts to stop movement

Questions

1 What is the attractive force between two objects?

2 What would happen to a spacecraft which ran out of fuel before it reached orbit?

3 On which planets are the Sun's gravitational force the greatest and the smallest?

4 Find out what a shooting star is.

5 What would be the weight of an astronaut if there was no gravity?

Space travel to the Moon

Successful space travel began with the launch of *Sputnik* in October 1957.

Sputnik was a **satellite** which orbited the Earth.

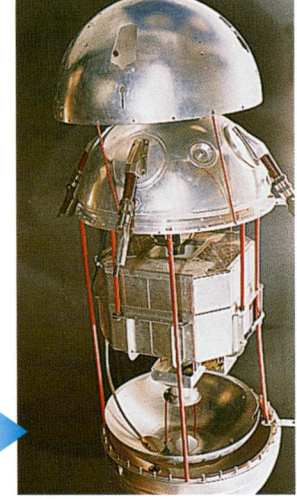

Figure 1
Sputnik

Figure 2 Saturn V rocket

The first man in space was a Russian, called Yuri Gagarin who entered space on 12th April 1961. He orbited the Earth only once and then returned. Sadly he was killed in an aircraft accident in 1968 and a crater on the Moon was named after him.

The first American in space was John Glenn who orbited the Earth in February 1962.

Race to the Moon

In the 1960s and 1970s America and the Soviet Union had a race to see which country could put a man on the Moon. This led to both countries spending a lot of time and resources on space travel.

In America the people who were sent into space were called **astronauts** and in Russia they were called **cosmonauts**.

In July 1969 America won the race by landing a man on the Moon. They had to spend about $30 billion to do it.

Man on the Moon!

When astronauts went to the Moon they used a large rocket called a *Saturn V* which launched the astronauts and their landing craft into space towards the Moon.

The rocket was made of three main stages (or sections) which burned all their fuel and then separated. The vast majority of the rocket was a large fuel tank!

Figure 3 The lunar landing module

Apollo 11 was launched on July 17th 1969 and reached the Moon three days later. The **lunar landing module** separated and landed on the Moon on the 20th July. Michael Collins was left in the **orbiter** to look after the craft so it could take them back to Earth.

Neil Armstrong and Buzz Aldrin then walked on to the Moon's surface. They set up science experiments, took photographs and collected rock samples. Neil Armstrong was on the surface for 2 hours and 13 minutes. They then returned to the orbiter and headed back to Earth.

Figure 4 Astronauts on the Moon

Figure 5 The scorched re-entry vehicle

When they reached the Earth they crawled into the re-entry vehicle which forced its way through the atmosphere and splashed down in the Pacific ocean on July 24th.

Six different teams made it to the Moon and returned safely. On one of the missions, *Apollo 13*, an oxygen tank on board split and the astronauts had to give up their mission and return to Earth.

They just managed to make it back safely.

Due to the way the rockets were designed, the only section that made it back was the re-entry vehicle. Every other part of the rocket was discarded or left in space.

The last mission to land astronauts on the Moon was *Apollo 17*. They landed in the South Ray and North Ray craters on April 20th 1972.

Key ideas

★ Rockets can launch large objects into space

★ *Saturn V* rockets were used to send astronauts to the moon

★ Large rockets are split into sections which are then discarded

Wordbank

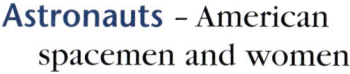

Satellite – object that orbits a planet

Astronauts – American spacemen and women

Cosmonauts – Soviet spacemen and women

Lunar Landing Module – vehicle which landed on the moon

Orbiter – command craft which orbited the moon

Questions

1 When was the first person launched into space?

2 Who was the first person in space?

3 What was the *Saturn V*?

4 Who were the first people to land on the moon?

5 When and where was the last mission to the moon?

6 How long did it take for the astronauts to reach the moon?

7 Make a labelled diagram of a *Saturn V* rocket about to be launched.

Space Travel – The next generation

Following the success of the Apollo missions, space travel was in a difficult position. Astronauts had already reached the Moon and the cost of travelling to other planets was unbelievably high. Space agencies began to investigate the regions of space around the Earth and in particular the use of artificial **satellites** to help us gather and send information.

The improvements in computing and technology in the past 20 years has meant that satellites can be used to direct television, telephone and radio signals to and from any place on Earth.

Figure 1 Satellites allow us to have telephone conversations with people on the other side of the world

There are also satellites which help us detect weather patterns and some can even photograph objects on the surface of the planet!

Most satellites are now launched by a **space shuttle**. Space shuttles are different from the *Saturn V* rockets in that sections of them can be re-used. This helps reduce the cost and allows for more missions to be launched.

The space shuttles use booster rockets to overcome the Earth's gravity and reach orbit. Once the fuel in the booster rockets is used up, they separate and fall into the sea. They are recovered and used again.

Figure 2 Space shuttles have huge booster rockets

The space shuttles are designed to store satellites and equipment in a cargo bay. When it is in the correct position above the Earth, it opens its payload doors and the satellite is launched into its required orbit. The shuttle then closes its doors and returns to Earth where it lands on a runway similar to that used by large jets.

Figure 3 These astronauts are on a 'space walk' to help launch the satellite

The first space shuttle was launched in 1981 and by the end of the year 2000 there had been more than 100 shuttle launches.

NASA is the organisation in the USA that is in control of the space programme. NASA controls the launch of all the shuttles and other rockets. It organises the research that scientists do to make space flight possible and it selects and trains the astronauts.

NASA has a large commitment to education and all the information that it gathers is available to the public.

Mars – here we come!

Mars is the nearest planet to Earth. Our first glimpse of the surface of Mars was in 1965 when a spacecraft flew past and sent photos back to Earth. Since then a number of unmanned spacecraft have landed on the surface.

In 1997, a vehicle which could explore the surface of Mars reached the planet after a seven-month journey. The robot rover, called *Sojourner*, saw Mars from the height of a house cat and sent back some spectacular photos of the planet surface over several days before it ran out of power.

Figure 4 The surface of Mars is cold, dry and rocky. It is called the 'red planet'

The next challenge will be to send humans to Mars. The cost of sending a manned spacecraft is so high that NASA is not planning a mission in the near future. NASA *will* send more rovers to explore the surface of Mars to find out about the composition of the planet, its atmosphere and weather.

The missions will also try to find evidence that life may once have existed on Mars! Scientists do not think that there will be any 'small green men' but there is a chance that there could be fossils of microbes or tiny organisms.

Key ideas

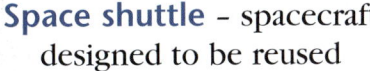

★ Satellites which orbit the Earth are used for communication
★ Space shuttles are used to launch satellites
★ Large sections of space shuttles can be reused
★ NASA is the US organisation that organises space exploration
★ Travel to other planets will be very expensive

Wordbank

Satellite – object that orbits a planet

Space shuttle – spacecraft designed to be reused

NASA – National Aeronautics and Space Administration

Questions

1 What do we use satellites for?

2 How is the space shuttle launched into space?

3 What does NASA stand for?

4 Why are NASA not considering a manned mission to Mars?

5 Space experiments

What would it be like to live in space?

If you travelled into space, the first thing you would notice is that you would start to float! This is because the gravitational 'pull' between you and the Earth becomes smaller the further you are away from the Earth. In deep space, there is no pull at all! There is no force to pull things down or to hold them to the floor. This is known as '**zero gravity**'.

How would our bodies feel if there was no gravity acting on us? Would we grow taller if there was no weight to pull us down? Would our muscles change if we did not have to support our weight?

Scientists have thought about such problems. Space travel will involve astronauts being in space for a very long time. They will have to learn to live in conditions which are very different from those we are used to on Earth.

In order to investigate these conditions scientists needed to do experiments to see exactly what happens.

Both the USA and Russia built laboratories in space. The USA built *Skylab* and Russia built *Mir*, both of which were space stations in which astronauts could do experiments in space.

Skylab orbited the Earth between May 1973 and July 1979 when it was allowed to crash into the Pacific Ocean. The main experiment was to find out how people would cope with living in a space environment. Three missions involved astronauts surviving in space conditions for long periods. The longest mission lasted 84 days.

Other experiments included taking spiders on board and observing what happens to the shape of their webs, and growing seeds in conditions of zero gravity to find out which way the roots and shoots would grow.

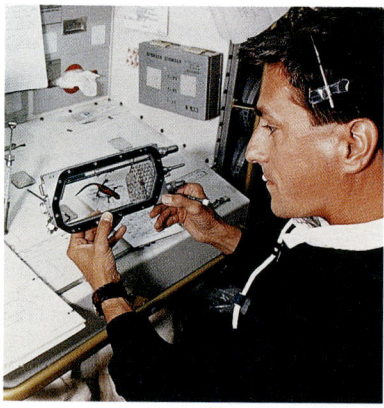

Figure 2 Astronaut investigating the effect of zero gravity on a newt

The Russian *Mir* space station was launched in February 1986 and was brought back to Earth in 2001.

Hubble Space Telescope

Probably the biggest number of experiments in space are those done by the Hubble Space Telescope (HST). It is a very large telescope that was taken into space by one of the space shuttles.

Figure 1 The Russian space station *Mir,* orbiting the Earth

Figure 3 The Hubble space telescope being launched from Shuttle Discovery

It is used to look at and examine stars that are very far away. It was put in orbit so astronomers could look at the light from stars and planets more clearly.

The Earth's atmosphere has many clouds and pieces of dust that float in the air. When we look at the stars, dust and pollution in the atmosphere can make the light from the stars very faint and difficult to see.

The Hubble Space Telescope does not have any of these problems because it orbits above the Earth's atmosphere. It can also take measurements 24 hours a day as there is no day or night time in space.

International Space Station

The International Space Station is being built by the USA and Russia. It will orbit the Earth and provide a laboratory for experiments in zero gravity. Medical and engineering companies are interested in doing experiments both inside and outside the space station!

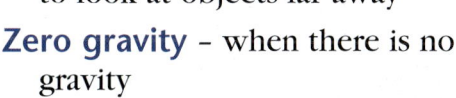

Figure 4 The International Space Station

Key ideas

★ There is no gravity in deep space
★ Space travel will involve people being in space for long periods of time
★ Living in space will have an effect on astronauts
★ Animals, chemicals and plants react differently to zero gravity
★ A telescope examines the light from distant objects

Wordbank

Telescope – an instrument used to look at objects far away
Zero gravity – when there is no gravity

Questions

1 What experiments did scientists do in their space stations?

2 Why do you think a spiders web has a different shape in space?

3 What are the advantages of having a telescope in space?

4 Can you think of two experiments you would like to do in space?

6 The United States of Matter

What goes THUMP.... SWISH.... SPLASH?

Someone diving off a springboard!

When you dive from a springboard you bounce off the board and it launches you into the air. The board feels hard on your feet and the air feels like wind blowing over your body. When you enter the water it makes a splash and you feel the water moving around your body.

Each different feeling is caused by the board, the air and the water. The board is a **solid**. The air is a **gas**. The water is a **liquid**.

Scientists call these the 'Three States of Matter'.

Everything on Earth is made of **matter**. Matter is the name for the materials from which everything is made – you, the table, the air around you, everything.

Figure 1 What are the three states of matter in this fizzy drink?

The glass is a solid.
The juice is a liquid.
The bubbles are a gas.

Solids

Solids have the following properties:

- Solids usually feel hard.
- Solids stay the same shape.
- Solids always take up the same space. This is called the **volume**.

Solids that keep their shape and volume are used to make things.

Figure 2 Solids are very useful

Liquids

Liquids have the following properties:

- Liquids take the shape of their container.

Think about when you pour a glass of water from a bottle into a glass. The water which was the shape of the bottle takes the shape of the glass. Pour the water in to another glass and it changes shape again!

- Liquids can change shape but they still have the same volume.

A carton of orange juice contains 250 millilitres. It does not matter whether the drink is in the carton, a glass or a measuring jug – the volume stays the same.

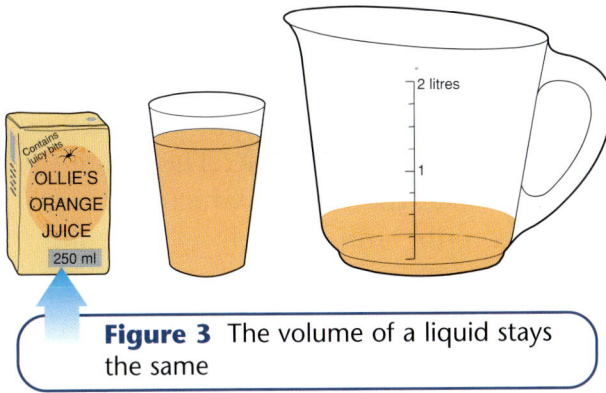

Figure 3 The volume of a liquid stays the same

Figure 4 The air takes the shape and volume of the balloon

There are lots of liquids but they all have these properties.

Gases

Gases have the following properties:

- Gases take up the same shape and volume of their container.

The shape of the balloon is dependant upon the type of balloon not the gas.

Gases are easily **compressed**. This means that more gas can be squeezed into a smaller space. This does not happen with solids and liquids. If the balloon is burst then the gas explodes out because it has been compressed. Normally compressed gases are stored in special containers to prevent explosions.

Key ideas

★ Materials exist in three states of matter – as **solids, liquids** and **gases**

★ Solids – have a fixed shape, a fixed volume, and cannot be easily compressed

★ Liquids – take up the shape of their container, have a fixed volume, and cannot be easily compressed

★ Gases – take up the shape of their container, have the volume of their container, and can be easily compressed

Wordbank

Volume – amount of space taken up by something

Compress – squeeze material into a smaller space

Questions

1 Here is a list of different substances. For each one write down if it is a solid, liquid or a gas.
   a) Bubbles in a fizzy drink.
   b) Dry sand running through your fingers.
   c) Ice cubes in a drink.
   d) Oil in frying pan.

2 Find out what scientists mean by the term 'matter'?

3 Survey your kitchen to find five solids, four liquids and three gases.

4 Write a 'sound story' that includes the sounds that are made by a solid, liquid and a gas.

5 Describe
   a) a solid
   b) a liquid
   c) a gas.

Is it possible to dig from Scotland to Australia?

The Earth is not solid. In fact only the surface of the Earth is made from solid rock. This is called the Earth's **crust** and it is only 10 kilometres thick. The crust surrounds the **mantle**. This is a very hot layer of rock – so hot that the rock has melted (1400°C). The **molten** (melted) rock of the mantle moves about under the crust. Great streams of molten rock flow slowly from place to place.

Deep inside the Earth, right at the centre, is the **core**. The core is extremely hot (4000°C) and is made of liquid iron.

The Earth's crust is a bit like the shell on a soft-boiled egg. It is very thin and hard and surrounds soft layers inside. The white of the egg is like the mantle which lies just under the crust and the yolk is a bit like the core in the centre.

The Earth's crust is more like a cracked eggshell. It is made up of a number of big pieces called **plates**, which fit together like the pieces of a giant jigsaw puzzle. The movement of the molten rock in the mantle can cause these plates to move. This disturbance can cause earthquakes and volcanic eruptions.

Figure 2 Earthquakes can cause a lot of damage

In some places the crust is very thin and cracked and the hot, molten rock can break through to the surface of the Earth.

crust

mantle

core

Figure 1 The layers inside the Earth

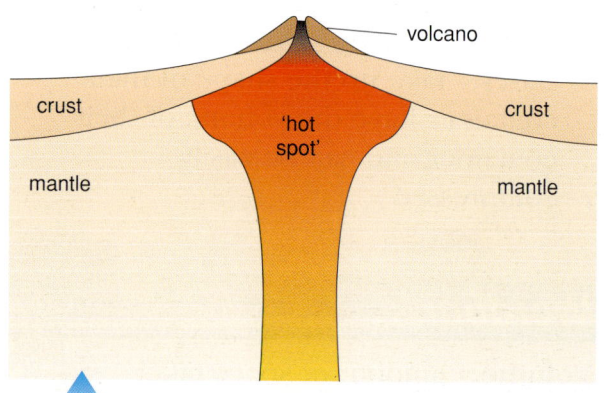

volcano

crust   crust

'hot spot'

mantle   mantle

Figure 3 A volcano is formed from molten rock in the mantle pushing up through the Earth's crust

The molten rock is under pressure, like the air in a balloon. When it finds a weak spot in the crust, it explodes out with great force. Smoke, fire and molten rock can all pour out forming a volcano. The molten rock produced by a volcano is called **lava**.

Figure 4 Volcanic eruptions can be spectacular!

Birth of an island

Volcanoes can appear on the sea floor as well as on land. Over many years, the lava from a sea floor volcano can build up to form an island. Hawaii is a volcanic island.

Edinburgh Castle sits on the top of what was once a volcano. Fortunately the volcano is now extinct, which means that it will no longer erupt.

Figure 5 Edinburgh Castle was built on top of an extinct volcano

Key ideas

★ The crust of the Earth is the thin outside layer, which consists of the land and the sea

★ The crust is made up of a number of very large plates, like a giant jigsaw puzzle

★ The mantle of the Earth is made up of molten rock

★ Volcanoes are formed when the mantle breaks through a weak part of the crust and hot molten rock pours out

Wordbank

Crust – the thin outside layer of the Earth

Mantle – the layer of molten rock beneath the crust

Core – the very centre of the Earth

Plates – the name for the sections of the crust, which move

Lava – molten rock produced by a volcano

Questions

1 Which is the thinnest layer – the crust, the mantle or the core of the Earth?

2 What is the mantle made up of?

3 What causes an earthquake?

4 How are volcanoes formed and why do they erupt?

5 What problems would you encounter if you tried to dig through to the centre of the Earth?

How rocks are made

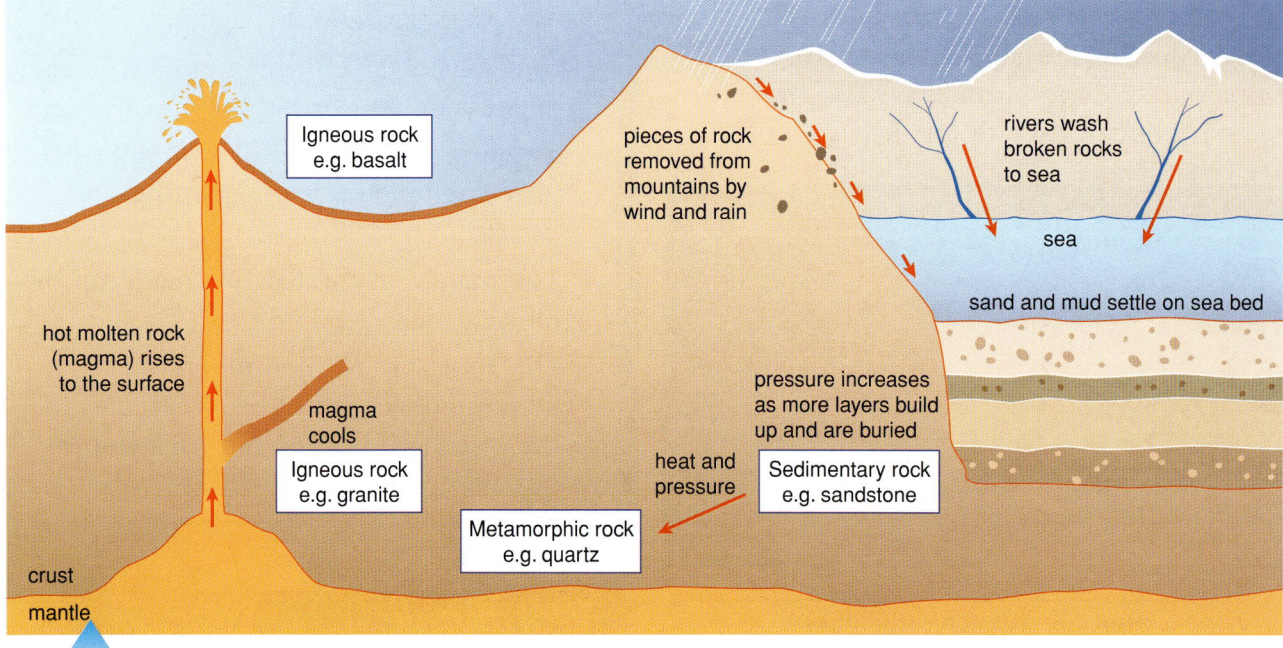

Igneous rock
e.g. basalt

pieces of rock
removed from
mountains by
wind and rain

rivers wash
broken rocks
to sea

sea

sand and mud settle on sea bed

hot molten rock
(magma) rises
to the surface

magma
cools

Igneous rock
e.g. granite

pressure increases
as more layers build
up and are buried

heat and
pressure

Sedimentary rock
e.g. sandstone

Metamorphic rock
e.g. quartz

crust

mantle

Figure 1 The rock cycle

Figure 2 Basalt is an igneous rock. It is formed when lava cools quickly, producing tiny crystals

The Earth is 4600 million years old. However no rocks as old as this have ever been found. This is because all the time, very slowly, old rocks are worn away and new rocks are being formed. This process is called **the rock cycle**.

The Earth's crust is made up of different kinds of rock of which there are three main types.

Igneous rock

The Earth's crust is a thin layer of cool, solid rock. Beneath the crust, the hot, molten rock in the mantle moves about. As it moves, the molten rock pushes its way to the surface through cracks and splits in the crust (Figure 1).

As it pushes its way into the crust the rock cools down and forms what is called **igneous rock**. As it cools, crystals are formed in the rock. The quicker the rock cools, the smaller the crystals that are formed.

Figure 3 Granite is an igneous rock made of large crystals. The large crystals formed because the molten rock cooled slowly under the surface

Sedimentary rock

Rivers and streams wash little pieces of rock down from the hills and mountains. This is called **erosion**. As they are carried along, the pieces of rock bump against the river bed and each other, causing the pieces to become even smaller. Some of the rock settles to the bottom of the river but the smallest particles of sand and mud may be carried all the way to the sea.

The very small pieces of sand and mud settle on the sea bed. Over thousands of years more sand and mud settle on top. As the layers grow thicker and thicker, they press down on the lower layers. This pressure is so great that these layers turn to rock. Rock that is formed like this is called **sedimentary rock**.

Figure 4 Sandstone is made from tiny grains of sand squeezed tightly together

Figure 5 It took millions of years for all these layers of sedimentary rock to form

Metamorphic rock

Over millions of years, the layers of sedimentary rock are buried deeper and deeper. They are squeezed by the layers above and heated from below by the hot core of the Earth. The pressure and heat changes the rock. Rocks that are formed like this are called **metamorphic rocks**.

Figure 6 Marble is a metamorphic rock. It is limestone that has been heated and squeezed in the Earth's crust

Key ideas

★ The rocks around us have been formed in one of three ways

★ Igneous rocks are formed when hot molten rock cools down and forms crystals

★ Sedimentary rocks form in layers as sand and small pieces of rock settle to the sea bed

★ When sedimentary rocks are buried, heated and squeezed they change into metamorphic rocks

★ The rocks are connected through the rock cycle, which occurs over millions of years

Wordbank

The rock cycle – process through which old rocks are worn away and new rocks are formed

Igneous – rock that is formed when the hot molten rock from the mantle cools in the crust

Sedimentary – rock that is formed when layers of sand and mud are squeezed

Metamorphic – rock that is formed when sedimentary rock is heated and squeezed

Erosion – movement of rock particles

Questions

1 What are the three main kinds of rock?

2 Which kind of rock is made by squeezing small grains of material together?

3 What kind of rock is limestone?

4 Describe one way in which rock is broken down into smaller pieces.

9 Weathering and erosion

The surface of the Earth is constantly changing. This may come as a surprise, as the hills, valleys and cliffs around you may not look any different now than when you were born. This is because the processes that change the surface of the Earth happen very slowly.

Weathering is the breaking down of rocks into smaller and smaller pieces. Rocks are broken down into boulders, which are broken down into gravel and so on.

rock → boulders → gravel → sand → silt → clay

The smaller the pieces of rock are, the easier they are moved. The movement of weathered rock is called **erosion**. Over thousands of years, weathering and erosion can have a huge effect on the landscape.

Figure 1 The Old Man of Hoy in the Orkney islands was formed by weathering and erosion of sandstone

Rocks can be broken down by temperature (heat and cold), the action of wind, water and chemicals. In general these can be broken down into two types: physical weathering and chemical weathering.

Physical weathering

When rocks are heated by the sun they **expand** (get bigger), and when they cool down they **contract** (get smaller). If heated and cooled often enough, the outer layer of rock will crack.

Wind action

Wind is sometimes strong enough to dislodge particles of sand from a rock. The sand may then be carried by the wind. If the sand hits another rock it will dislodge even more particles, causing the rock to wear away.

Action of water

A most unusual property of water is that when it freezes, it expands. During the winter this can cause burst water pipes!

Water enters tiny cracks in rocks. When the water freezes, it expands and pushes the rock apart. When this is repeated many times it causes the rock to break.

Water in streams, rivers and the sea break rocks into smaller and smaller pieces. The rock debris is often transported hundreds of miles away.

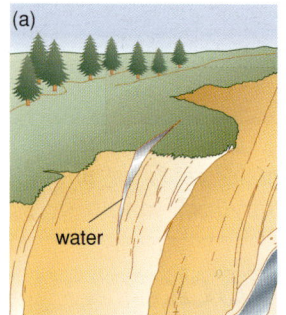
(a) water

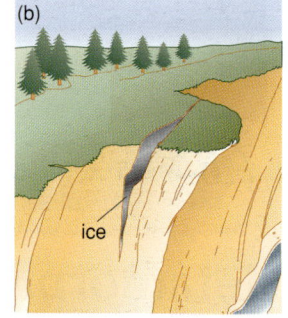
(b) ice

(c)

Figure 2 a) Water fills cracks in rocks b) The water freezes and expands, causing the crack to become wider until c) the rock splits

Water erosion can be very important in shaping the landscape.

Figure 3 The Colorado River in the USA has carved out the Grand Canyon which is 1.5 km deep!

Chemical weathering

Some chemicals dissolve in water and make it acidic. Burning fossil fuels can make carbon dioxide and sulphur dioxide. Acid rain is produced when these gases dissolve in rain water.

Acid rain attacks rock and dissolves it. Limestone is easily dissolved in rain water and can quickly erode.

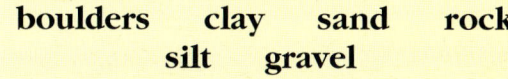

Figure 4 Acid rain has eroded this statue

Over many years, weathering and erosion have shaped the landscape. Some rocks erode more quickly than others. The famous white cliffs of Dover, which are sedimentary rocks are eroded quite quickly. Some cliffs in Scotland are eroded quite slowly.

Key ideas

★ Rock is broken down into smaller pieces by weathering and moved by erosion

★ Temperature, wind, water and chemicals each help to weather and erode rock

★ Different rocks erode at different rates

★ Over many years weathering and erosion shape the landscape

Wordbank

Weathering – rock being broken down into smaller pieces

Erosion – movement of weathered rock

Expand – to become bigger

Contract – to become smaller

Questions

1 What is meant by weathering?

2 What is meant by erosion?

3 Sort these into the correct order starting with the largest:

   boulders   clay   sand   rock
   silt   gravel

4 List four ways that rock can weather.

5 Describe how water can help to weather rock.

6 Describe how carbon dioxide and sulphur dioxide can help to weather rock.

10   *The formation of soil*

Soil covers most of the land surface of the Earth. Plants depend on the soil for water and nutrients. Soils affect what plants grow where. Farmers rely on soils for healthy crops.

Soils are formed from the **weathering** of the **bedrock** underneath. The bedrock is broken down into smaller particles of sand, silt and clay. Soils take a long time to form – hundreds or maybe even many thousands of years.

Soil formation is much faster when living things colonise the weathered rock.

Plant roots break rock apart and allow air into the soil. Burrowing animals move soil about and create air spaces in the soil. Air helps soil formation because oxygen reacts with (**oxidises**) the rock fragments and breaks them down. Tiny organisms in the soil release carbon dioxide, which forms acid with the water in the soil. The acid accelerates weathering.

Soil profile

Soil is made up of a number of layers (Figure 1). These are described as a soil profile.

If you look closely you will see soil is made up of many living and non-living parts.

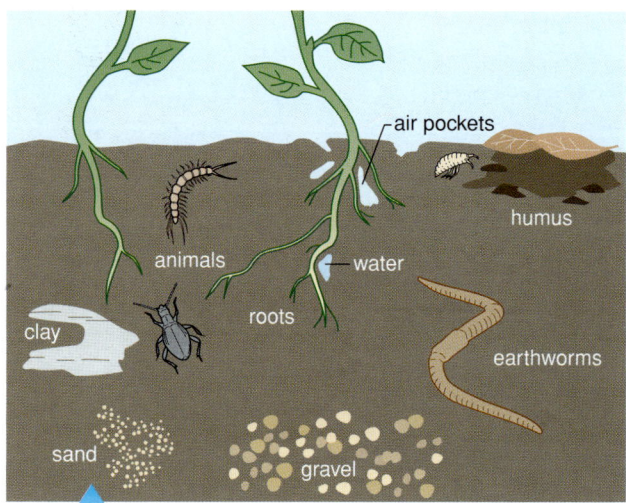

Figure 2 Soil is made up of living and non-living parts

Natural recycling

After living things die, their bodies begin to decay. Bacteria and fungi in the soil **decompose** this material to **humus**. Humus does not break down easily. It is a natural fertiliser and helps to hold the soil particles together. Fertile soils contain a lot of humus.

Plant material and creatures are found in the **surface layer.**

Top soil is the most fertile part of the soil and contains air, soil crumbs and water.

Sub soil contains particles which are less well weathered. It contains fewer living things.

Bedrock is weathered slowly to produce soil. Different types of soil are produced from different types of bedrock.

Figure 1 A soil profile

Gardeners put vegetable waste and weeds onto a **compost** heap. Fungi and bacteria in the compost heap decompose this into humus, which the gardener returns to the soil. Living things that help in the process of decay are called decomposers, they recycle useful material back into the soil.

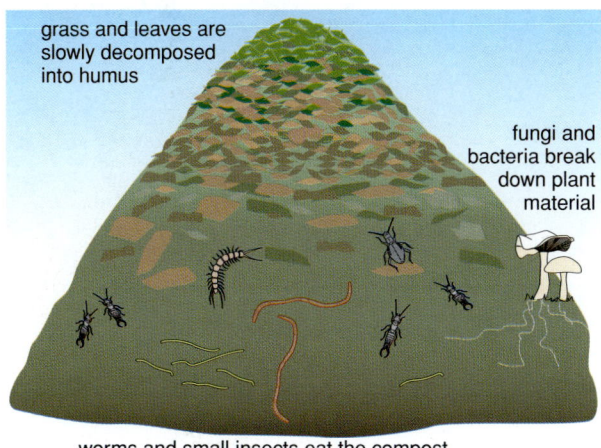

grass and leaves are slowly decomposed into humus

fungi and bacteria break down plant material

worms and small insects eat the compost and help the breakdown to humus

Figure 3 A compost heap

Soil types

Soils may have different balances of minerals and particles because they are formed from the weathering of different bedrock or contain different living things. Near the coast the soil often contains a lot of sand.

Sandy soils drain quickly, clay soils are heavy and stick to your boots. The best soils are called **loams** - they have a balance of sand and clay.

Figure 4 These wildflowers are growing on a sandy soil called Machair

Questions

1

Make a labelled diagram of this soil. Make a short note to describe each layer.

2 How do plants help soil formation?

3 Name and describe three types of soil.

11 Crust materials

Humans have used materials from the Earth's crust for thousands of years.

Rocks

Earliest man used rocks to make tools. This was called the Stone Age.

Figure 1 Stone was difficult to shape

We still use rocks today. Slate is a metamorphic rock, which can be split into flat slabs. These are then used to cover the roof of a house. Other types of rock, such as sandstone, can be used as building blocks. Lots of old buildings were made from sandstone. Granite is an igneous rock, which was used to make hard-wearing cobbles for streets.

Figure 2 Rocks used for building

Metals

Most rocks are made from a mixture of materials. Some rocks contain metals mixed with other materials. These are called **ores**.

In the Bronze Age metals were obtained by heating ores in fires to separate the metal from the rock. Bronze was much easier to shape into useful instruments than stone.

Figure 3 Bronze is a mixture of copper and tin

Even later came the Iron Age. By heating a different ore to an even higher temperature with coke (a type of coal) iron could be obtained. Iron is much harder than bronze and could be used to make many useful tools.

Figure 4 Making iron needs much higher temperatures

Some metals are found naturally in the Earth and need little or no treatment. These metals can be dug directly out of the Earth crust. These metals are called precious metals and include gold and silver.

Silicon

Another material which is plentiful in the Earths' crust, is **silicon**. This chemical is often found combined with oxygen. The common name for this compound is sand. Sand is a very useful substance as it is very hard-wearing and does not dissolve in water.

Sand can also be turned into glass by heating to a very high temperature.

Figure 5 Glass-blowing at Caithness Glass

Clay

Clay is another material which contains silicon. Clay can be formed into regular shapes and when baked in special ovens can make bricks for modern buildings or pots for containers.

Fuels

Fossil fuels such as coal, oil and gas all contain the element carbon. They are formed from the remains of tiny animals and plants. Over millions of years their bodies changed to coal, oil or gas.

Fuels can be burned to provide us with energy. Most of the electricity we use is generated from the burning of fossil fuels in power stations.

Wood is used for building and for furniture, and as a fuel in many poorer countries.

Oil is used to make petrol for cars and lorries. It is also used to make plastics and many other useful chemicals.

Key ideas

★ The Earth's crust contains many materials which we use

★ Most useful materials are not found naturally but are combined together

★ Ores are rocks which can be treated to produce metals

★ Fossil fuels are based mainly on the element carbon

Wordbank

Ores – rocks which contain metals combined with other materials

Silicon – chemical found in sand and clay

Fossil fuel – energy source based on the element carbon

Questions

1 Name two uses for natural materials extracted from the Earth.

2 What is done to iron ore to make the pure metal?

3 What is the main chemical found in glass?

4 Why are bricks made into regular shapes before building a wall?

5 Name three fossil fuels.

6 Look in the room around you. Try to identify as many things as possible which are made from:

   a) rock
   b) metal
   c) wood
   d) plastic.

23

Properties of materials

The natural materials which we extract from the Earth's crust have properties which make them useful. Most materials are changed using technology to make them even more useful. For example, we convert oil to petrol to use as fuel for cars.

Some properties which we might consider useful are:

Strength

Some materials are strong. This allows them to carry a heavy load.

Steel and concrete buildings are very strong. Bridges over motorways are made of steel and concrete because they have to carry the weight of the traffic.

Figure 1 This bridge was built with reinforced concrete

Flexibility

Plastic wrappings around foods from the supermarket have to be flexible to fit the shape of the food. But they must also be strong to prevent them tearing open and the food being exposed.

Egg boxes are designed to prevent damage to the eggs. In this case we do not want the material to be flexible.

Figure 2 Food packaging is carefully chosen

Durability

Slate is a natural material used to tile the roofs of houses as it does not wear away easily by the action of the weather. Durable means that once in place it will last for a very long time.

Figure 3 Slate is used for roof tiles

Resistance to corrosion

We normally think about corrosion as affecting metals. For example if iron is left open to air and water it will rust. Rusting is the special name given to the corrosion of iron.

If we need a strong material, which does not rust we would make a special type of iron called steel. This is a man-made material. Stainless steel is used to make cutlery because we do not want it to corrode.

Figure 4 Stainless steel is used for cutlery. It is strong and does not react with food

Flammability

Some materials burn and provide heat energy. Other materials do not burn.

In a gas cooker the gas is the fuel which burns to provide heat energy. The cooking pot, which is made from glass, does not burn.

Figure 5 Some materials are flammable and others are not

Elasticity

Some materials are used because they are elastic. Elastic materials can stretch and return to their original shape.

Figure 6 Liz McColgan wears clothes made from an elastic material called Lycra

Elastic fabrics are used because they allow easier movement.

Key ideas

★ Different materials have different properties

★ By combining materials the properties can change

★ Common properties include strength, flexibility, resistance to corrosion, flammability and elasticity

Wordbank

Strength – does it break easily?

Flexibility – can its shape be changed without it breaking?

Durability – does it wear away or dissolve?

Corrosion – does it breakdown easily?

Flammability – will it burn easily?

Elasticity – can it stretch and return to its original shape?

Questions

1 Name four common properties of materials.

2 Which properties are important for making a fence around a garden?

3 Name a material which is resistant to corrosion.

4 When might it be a good thing for a material to break easily?

5 A sofa found in your living room is treated with special chemicals to make it non flammable. Why is this a good idea?

6 An archer uses a bow and arrow. What properties does the bow have?

13 It's a Gas!

The Earth is surrounded by a blanket of gas, which we call the atmosphere.

Factfile

The atmosphere:

➤ reaches over 500 kilometres from the surface of the Earth

➤ contains a mixture of gases including nitrogen, oxygen and many others

➤ absorbs energy from the Earth

➤ recycles water and other chemicals

➤ protects us from the **vacuum** of space and harmful radiation from the Sun.

the atmosphere is a thin layer of air

Figure 1 The atmosphere

Nitrogen (N$_2$)

Discovered in 1772 by a scientist in Scotland.

Nearly all of the atmosphere is made of nitrogen (about 78%). You can probably guess some of its properties since the air around you is mostly nitrogen. It is colourless and does not have a smell.

Oxygen (O$_2$)

Discovered in 1774 by a scientist in England.

The second most abundant gas in the atmosphere is oxygen (nearly 21%).

We breathe in oxygen to live and it allows things to burn. Because oxygen is a very **reactive** gas nearly half of the Earth's crust contains substances that contain oxygen.

Argon (Ar)

Discovered in 1894 in Scotland.

Argon makes up most of the rest of the atmosphere (about 1%). It does not react with other materials. Gases that do not react with other materials are known as **inert** or **noble** gases.

Figure 2 The gas in light bulbs is argon. Argon is used because it is unreactive

Water (H$_2$O)

Water vapour is a gas that is present in the atmosphere. Much of our weather involves water being present in the atmosphere. The water cycle shows how water can fall as rain, hail or snow. Sometimes the air feels very **humid** and this usually means that a lot of water vapour is in the air and we feel quite sticky.

Figure 3 Water vapour in the atmosphere can be in the form of clouds

Ozone (O₃)

Most ozone is found in the upper atmosphere. Ozone is colourless and smells a bit like the swimming pool. It is formed when lightning reacts with oxygen (O_2). Ozone in the atmosphere protects living things from harmful radiation from the Sun.

Carbon dioxide (CO₂)

Carbon dioxide is also a colourless gas. Carbon dioxide is present in the atmosphere and is made by living things.

Figure 4 The bubbles in fizzy drinks are carbon dioxide

Hydrogen (H₂)

Discovered in 1766 by a scientist in England.

Hydrogen is a colourless gas and it is very reactive. It is the lightest substance known and is the most abundant substance in the universe. Stars are made, mostly, from hydrogen.

Figure 5 Hydrogen was used in the Hindenberg airship. It exploded when the hydrogen caught fire

Key ideas

★ The atmosphere is a mixture of gases

★ Space contains no gas

★ The atmosphere protects us from space

★ Gases can be reactive or unreactive

Wordbank

Vacuum – space where no gases are found

Reactive – able to change into another substance by a chemical reaction

Inert – not reactive with other chemicals

Noble gas – inert gas

Humid – moist air

Questions

1 Make a table to list the gases found in the atmosphere. Give the symbol of each gas.

2 Name the two gases that were discovered in Scotland.

3 Name all the gases that were discovered in England.

4 What two names can be used to indicate that gases do not react chemically with other materials?

5 Find out more about the following:

   troposphere, stratosphere, ozone hole

   and the scientists that discovered each of the gases.

14 Using Gases!

Atmospheric gases are widely used to help us in all aspects of our lives.

Extracting gases from the air

This is how gas is extracted from the air.

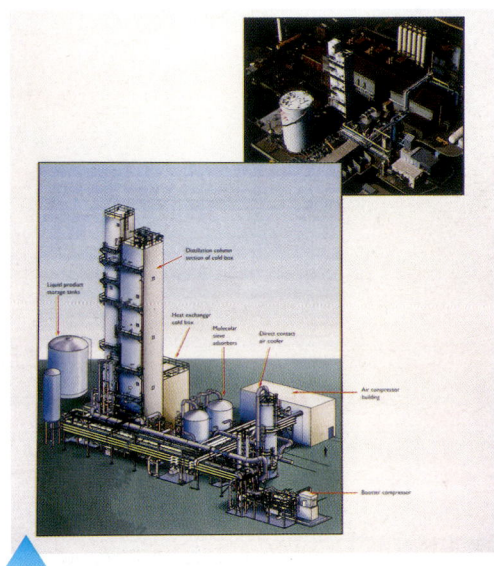

Figure 1 An air extraction plant

Atmospheric gases (oxygen, nitrogen, argon and the other noble gases, namely neon, krypton and xenon) are obtained from special air extraction plants. Air is **compressed** – this is just like squeezing air inside a bicycle pump – then the compressed air is cooled to such a low temperature that it turns into a liquid.

Use in hospitals

Oxygen

Pure oxygen is used in hospitals to help patients recover from certain illnesses.

The air around us, which we breathe in, contains 21% oxygen. Air is taken into the lungs, and oxygen is absorbed by the bloodstream and carried around the body.

When 100% oxygen is breathed, there is an increase in the amount of oxygen carried around the body. This extra oxygen helps patients who are having difficulty breathing, for example patients suffering from lung disease.

Lasers

Lasers are intense beams of light that can be focussed on very small areas. They can be used as a kind of knife by surgeons when they are carrying out operations. Lasers use gases, such as argon or helium. These unreactive gases help to pinpoint the effect of the laser on a small area. Lasers can be used to seal tiny holes in blood vessels and to destroy diseased tissue which is surrounded by healthy tissue.

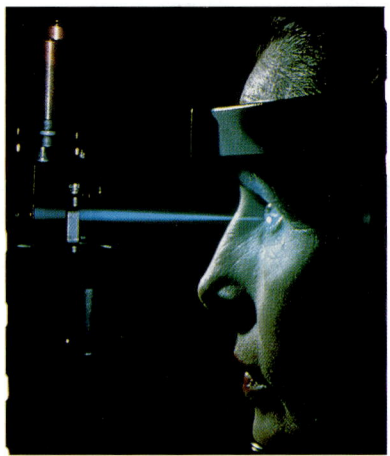

Figure 2 Many people have benefited from eye operations where the surgeon used lasers

Use in the food industry

The bubbles that make soft drinks fizzy are carbon dioxide. Carbon dioxide gas is compressed and forced into the liquid.

Beer and champagne fizz because they are made by yeast. Yeast produces lots of carbon dioxide, which becomes trapped in the bottle and is released when you take off the cork.

Use in sport

Scuba divers need to breathe air when they are underwater. They carry tanks on their back which contain compressed air. Divers must be careful to watch how long they have stayed under the water in case they run out of air.

Figure 3 Scuba divers carry tanks containing compressed air

Use in industry

Oxygen helps things burn. When very high temperatures are needed extra oxygen is supplied. By burning a fuel with extra oxygen, enough heat is produced to melt metals.

Carbon dioxide gas is often used in fire extinguishers. It prevents the oxygen reaching the burning material and stops it burning.

Figure 4 This instrument can be used to weld metals together

Use as fuels

LOX (liquid oxygen) and **hydrazine** (a chemical that releases hydrogen gas) are used as rocket fuels. They are an explosive mixture and must be treated very carefully before the space shuttle takes off.

Key ideas

★ Gases are widely used by mankind
★ Gases have different properties which affects how they are used

Wordbank

Compress – being squeezed into a smaller space

Laser – intense beam of light

LOX – liquid oxygen used as rocket fuel

Hydrazine – chemical that releases hydrogen gas in rockets

Questions

1 Name five uses of gases.

2 Name four noble gases.

3 Name three uses of oxygen.

4 Name two uses of carbon dioxide.

5 Name one use of argon.

6 Why does the gas used in cookers have a smelling agent added to it?

A **mixture** is two substances that are mixed together but not joined. Both substances stay the same and no new substance is formed.

When you mix two solids together, you can still see each one. Neither solid has changed – they still look the same. For example, when sand is mixed with small stones, you can still see the grains of sand amongst the stones.

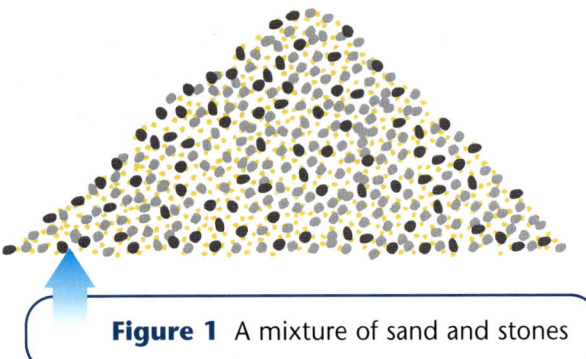

Figure 1 A mixture of sand and stones

When sugar grains and coffee granules are mixed together, they do not change. You can still see the white grains of sugar amongst the brown coffee granules.

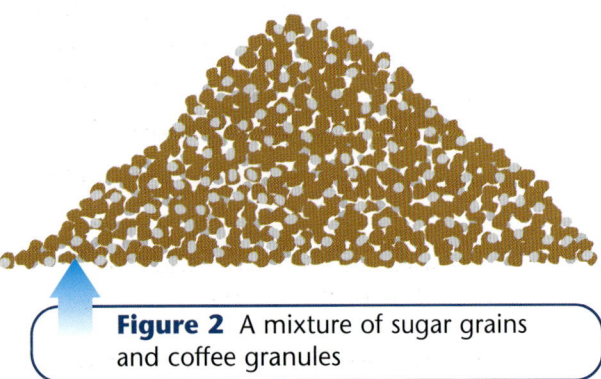

Figure 2 A mixture of sugar grains and coffee granules

There are lots of mixtures around us. Soil is a mixture of gravel, sand, clay and humus. Sometimes it is difficult to see the different substances that make up some mixtures. For example, the air we breathe is a mixture of gases but we cannot see the different gases. Fizzy drinks are mixtures of flavoured syrup, water and carbon dioxide (to make it fizz).

Going, going gone . . . or is it?

Sometimes you cannot see the different substances in a mixture but you can tell that they are there in other ways. If you mix sugar and water together, the sugar seems to disappear. If you taste the water, it tastes sweet and you know that the sugar is still there. The sugar has not disappeared; it has **dissolved** in the water. This type of mixture is called a **solution**.

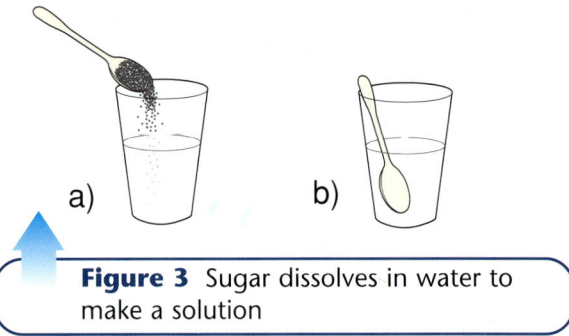

a)   b)

Figure 3 Sugar dissolves in water to make a solution

The solid that is dissolved (the sugar) is called the **solute** and the liquid (the water) is the **solvent**.

When a substance is dissolved it is broken down into such tiny particles that they cannot be seen. If the solute dissolves completely, the solution should be **transparent** (see-through) although it may be coloured. When jelly cubes are dissolved in water, the solution will be transparent but will be coloured.

Figure 4 Dissolving jelly

We normally use *hot* water when we are making jelly because it helps the jelly to dissolve more quickly.

Some substances dissolve more easily than others. We say that they are more **soluble**. For example salt is much more soluble than sand.

Concentrate!

When you dissolve jelly in water and if you taste the water, it will have the same flavour as the jelly. The more jelly cubes you use, the stronger or more **concentrated** the solution will be. A solution with only a small amount of jelly will be a **weak** solution.

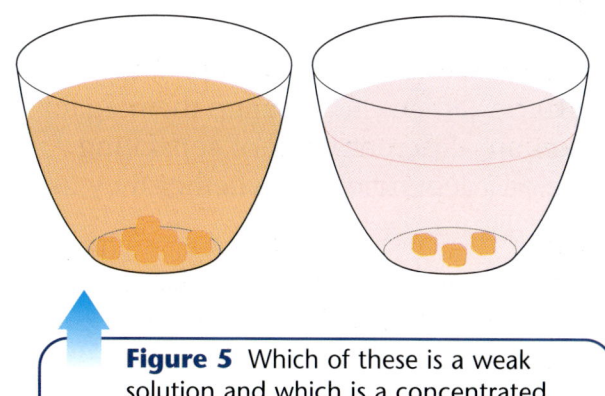

Figure 5 Which of these is a weak solution and which is a concentrated solution? How can you tell?

You can also make a solution weaker by adding more solvent. The more water we add to the jelly, the more we **dilute** the solution.

Key ideas

★ Substances in a **mixture** are not joined together

★ A **solution** is a special kind of mixture in which a solid is dissolved in a liquid

★ When a solid is dissolved in a liquid, the solid is the **solute** and the liquid is the **solvent**

★ A **concentrated** solution can be **diluted** by adding more of the solvent

Wordbank

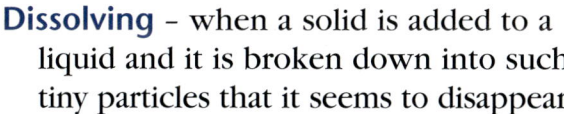

Mixture – two (or more) substances which are mixed together but not joined

Dissolving – when a solid is added to a liquid and it is broken down into such tiny particles that it seems to disappear

Solution – a liquid with another substance dissolved in it

Solute – the material that dissolves

Solvent – the substance it dissolves in

Questions

1 Copy and put each word in the correct space:
solution solute solvent liquid weak concentrated

A _____ is when you put a solid into a _____ and it dissolves. In a solution of salt and water the salt is the _____ and the water is the _____. If you put a lot of salt in, you have a _____ solution. If you put a small amount in, you will get a _____ solution.

2 Make a list of the substances you know that will dissolve in water.

3 Name the solute and the solvent in the following solutions:
a) salt dissolved in water
b) water with carbon dioxide dissolved in it
c) blue ink dissolved in cleaning fluid
d) tea dissolved in hot water
e) water with an aspirin dissolved in it

16 *Unmixing it!*

Once materials have been mixed together, it can be difficult to separate them again. There are different ways of separating materials depending on whether they are solids, liquids or gases.

Separating solids

One way of separating mixtures of solids is by **sieving**. For example, if you wanted to separate gravel from sand, a sieve would be very useful. The sieve would need to have holes small enough to let the sand through but not the small stones. The stones are trapped in the sieve while the sand passes through.

A mixture of different sizes of stone can be sorted using a series of sieves:

big stones

small stones

gravel

sand

Figure 1 A series of sieves with different sized holes allows you to separate stones of different sizes

Separating solids from liquids

A **filter** is a kind of sieve that lets liquid through but not solids.

One way of making a cup of coffee is by pouring hot water over ground coffee beans. The hot water dissolves some of the coffee but most of the granules are too large to dissolve. The mixture of water and coffee is poured through a paper filter. The liquid coffee passes through the filter but the coffee grounds are left behind in the paper.

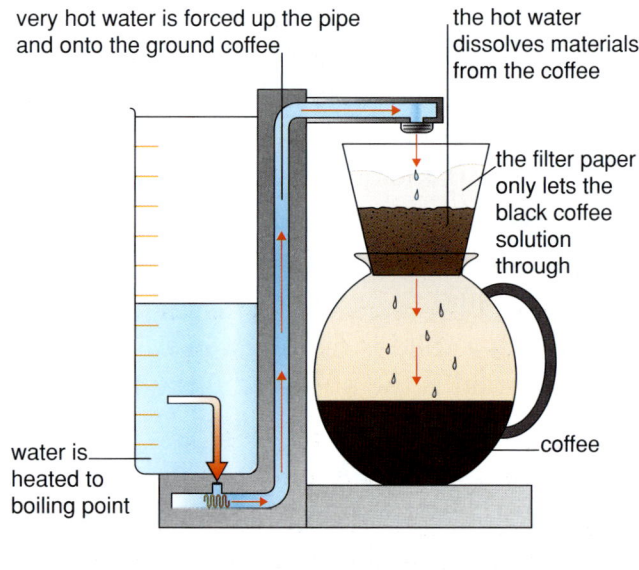

very hot water is forced up the pipe and onto the ground coffee

the hot water dissolves materials from the coffee

the filter paper only lets the black coffee solution through

water is heated to boiling point

coffee

Figure 2 Making filter coffee

The coffee that passes through the filter into the jug is a solution of hot water and coffee. The filter cannot separate the solvent (the water) from the solute (the dissolved coffee). The particles of coffee in the solution are so small that they just pass right through the filter paper with the water.

Separating substances in a solution

There are ways of separating the substances in a solution. Salt dissolves in water to produce a solution. You can get the salt back if you can get rid of the water.

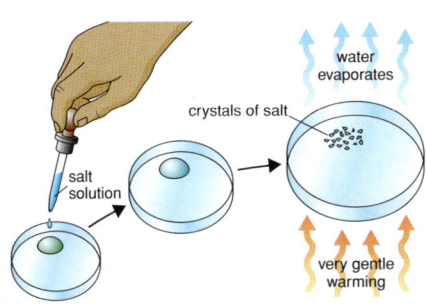

Figure 3 Salt crystals are formed when water evaporates from salt water

If you leave the dish of salt water sitting on the window sill, the water will **evaporate**. When water evaporates, tiny particles of water escape from the dish into the air. The salt is left behind in the dish.

This method is used to get salt from sea water. Sea water is a mixture of water and salt. In hot countries, sea water is poured into large, shallow ponds. The wind and the heat from the Sun evaporate the water, leaving the salt behind. It is then collected, cleaned and sold.

Figure 4 Evaporation is used to get salt from sea water

Key ideas

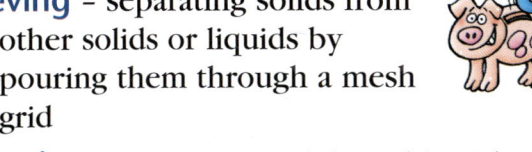

★ A **sieve** can be used to separate mixtures of solids of different sizes

★ A **filter** can be used to separate mixtures of liquids and solids

★ A solute can be recovered from a solution by **evaporating** the solvent

Wordbank

Sieving – separating solids from other solids or liquids by pouring them through a mesh grid

Filtering – separating solids and liquids by pouring them through paper or tightly woven material

Evaporating – removing the water from a solution to leave you with the solute

Questions

1 What might you separate using a sieve?

2 Sieving, filtering and evaporating are all methods of separating materials. Which one separates the substances in a solution?

3 a) How could you get back the sugar from a solution of sugar and water?
   b) What happens to the water?

4 What is the purpose of a bag in a tea bag?

17 Burning

For thousands of years people have burned wood, coal and oil in fires. Fires were, and still are used to provide heat for warmth and for cooking.

Materials, such as wood, coal and oil, which we burn to provide heat and light are called **fuels**.

Materials that can burn easily are known as '**flammable**'. Confusingly they can also be called '**inflammable**'. We have to be careful where flammable materials are stored, just in case a fire occurs.

Figure 1 This symbol tells us that the material is flammable

What causes fire?

Fires generally do not happen easily. The conditions need to be right in order for a fire to start. We need three things to start a fire:

1 fuel (flammable material)

2 heat

3 oxygen.

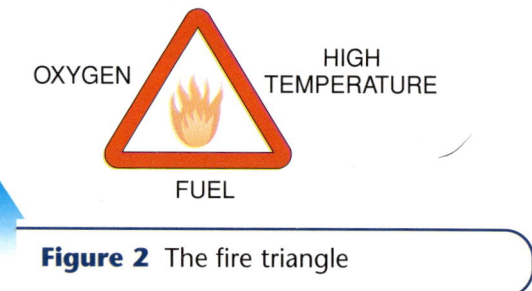

Figure 2 The fire triangle

If we have all three of these things, for example dry grass on a hot day, then there is a chance that a fire could start. If we don't have all three then a fire will not start.

Figure 3 A forest fire

What happens when things burn?

The most obvious thing that we notice when a substance burns is that it gives out heat and light.

Fuels have a lot of energy stored 'inside' them. When fuels are burned the energy 'inside' them is released and this is why fires give out heat and light. When all the energy inside the material has been used up the fires go out.

When coal burns it combines with oxygen in the air and a new substance is formed. The coal is also changed into a different substance. This is why things look different before and after they have burned.

No fire without smoke?

Most materials give off smoke and fumes when they burn. The smoke contains new substances that are formed when the material is burned.

The smoke and fumes from burning fuels can affect the environment.

Figure 5 Which of these has been burned and which has not? How can you tell?

Where has all the charcoal gone?

Figure 6 Smoke and fumes from blazing oil fields pollutes the environment

Key ideas

★ Flammable and inflammable means 'can burn easily'

★ Burning releases energy from inside the material

★ When a substance is burned it combines with oxygen and a new substance is formed

★ Fuels are substances that we burn to release heat and light energy

Questions

1 List five things in your classroom that can burn easily.

2 What three things do you need for a fire to start?

3 Which gas from the air is used when things burn?

4 Why are nightgowns made from non-flammable materials?

5 Why do things not burn underwater?

Wordbank

Fuel – a material which gives out lots of heat and light when it burns

Flammable – can burn easily

Inflammable – can burn easily

Burning fossil fuels

When fuels burn they combine with oxygen and new substances are formed. At the same time, energy is released from the fuel as heat and light. Most materials give off smoke and fumes when they burn.

The most common fuels are coal, oil and gas. These are called **fossil fuels**. We burn fossil fuels and use the energy they give out for transport and to generate electricity.

Fossil fuels for electricity

Power stations, factories and many homes burn large amounts of coal. Power stations use the heat energy released by the coal to convert water to steam. The steam then drives a turbine which generates electricity. We use the electricity in our homes, schools and in industry.

Figure 1 This power station burns large amounts of coal. As a result it produces large amounts of smoke and fumes

Fossil fuels for transport

Think about it! Almost every car and bus in the world burns some form of oil or petrol.

In city centres the air can become badly **polluted** due to the exhausts of all the cars and buses which release smoke and waste into the atmosphere.

Figure 2 The burning of oil and petrol in car engines produces smog which 'hangs' over cities such as Denver, U.S.A.

Harming the environment

When fossil fuels burn they produce smoke and gases, including carbon dioxide. All this waste released into the atmosphere can be harmful to our environment and to us!

The dust produced by burning can cause buildings to become dirty and discoloured and if people breathe in a lot of the dust it can cause coughing and lead to lung problems.

Figure 3 This traffic officer wears a protective mask

Fossil fuels contain sulphur. When coal burns, sulphur combines with oxygen to produce sulphur dioxide. Sulphur dioxide combines with water vapour in the atmosphere and falls as **acid rain**.

Acid rain affects rivers and lakes and can damage animals and plants living in water. Acid rain affects trees and buildings too. The stonework of many historic buildings is being destroyed by acid rain.

The problem of acid rain does not just affect the area around power stations. Winds can carry acid rain clouds many miles from where the fossil fuels are burned.

Figure 4 These trees in Norway are being destroyed by acid rain

Many scientists think that carbon dioxide produced by the burning of fossil fuels is contributing to a change in the planet's climate known as **global warming**.

What can we do?

The problem of pollution caused by the burning of fossil fuels is likely to increase as we use more and more electricity and drive more cars. We can try and reduce the amount of fuel that we burn by using less electricity and not driving our cars as much. If we use less fuel we can save ourselves money and also help protect the environment.

If we recycle more it means that we do not need to use fuel to make the item and this will in turn reduce our need for fuel.

Key ideas

★ We rely heavily on burning fossil fuels to provide the electricity we use in our everyday lives

★ Burning fossil fuels releases gases into the atmosphere

★ These gases cause harm to the environment

★ If we reduce the amount of fuel we burn we can help the environment

Wordbank

Fossil fuels – non-renewable fuels, such as coal, oil and gas

Pollution – waste produced by humans which is released into the environment

Global warming – rise in the temperature of the Earth caused by increased carbon dioxide in the environment

Acid rain – rain which contains sulphur dioxide, making it acidic

Questions

1 Why are coal, oil and gas known as fossil fuels?

2 What gases are made when fossil fuels burn?

3 How could we be more environmentally friendly?

4 List four things you could do in school that would mean you could use less fuel.

The atmosphere of the Earth is under threat. The atmosphere is made up of different gases but the amounts of these gases are changing. This is worrying many scientists and people.

The level of carbon dioxide has doubled over the last 100 years. This increase has been largely brought about by the enormous amounts of **fossil fuels**, such as coal, oil and gas, which are burned in power stations and in cars.

A delicate balance

When the Earth was first formed there was very little oxygen in the atmosphere. Over millions of years our atmosphere has been changed by green plants!

Green plants remove carbon dioxide from the atmosphere. They use it to make their own food in a special process called **photosynthesis**. During this process oxygen gas is released into the atmosphere.

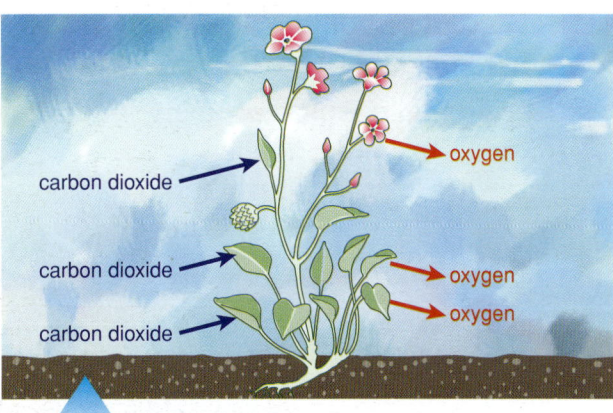

Figure 1 Green plants take in carbon dioxide and release oxygen during photosynthesis

Animals produce carbon dioxide when they breathe. There is a balance between the carbon dioxide produced by animals and the carbon dioxide taken in by plants.

Without green plants we would die as there would be no the oxygen to breathe.

Tipping the balance

In some parts of the world many millions of kilometres of forests are being cut down every year. Green parts of the countryside are having more and more houses built on them. This means there are fewer green plants to remove carbon dioxide and to replenish the atmosphere with oxygen.

Figure 2 Large areas of rainforest are being cut down and burnt

The balance between carbon dioxide and oxygen in the atmosphere is changing.

Why is carbon dioxide causing such concern?

Many scientists believe that carbon dioxide is causing a small increase in the temperature of our planet.

The atmosphere acts like a blanket around the Earth. It prevents heat escaping into space. Without the atmosphere the Earth would be colder. Carbon dioxide collects in the atmosphere and acts like an extra thick blanket. Because of it, the Earth is becoming warmer. This gradual change in temperature is called **global warming**.

Global warming may cause major problems if the polar ice caps melt. Low-lying areas in Scotland could be flooded due to the increase in the amount of water caused by the melting ice.

What can we do about it?

Many environmental groups are very worried about the damage being done to the atmosphere and other areas of the environment.

Those countries which have been industrialised for many years, such as the UK and the rest of Europe, Russia, the USA, Canada, Japan and Australia, are the main sources of this increase in carbon dioxide. However many more countries are now becoming industrialised which will lead to more polluting gases being released into the atmosphere.

This issue needs to be addressed now. The question is how can we bring about a reduction in carbon dioxide gas?

The main answer is to reduce the amount of fossil fuel used. We should use more environmentally friendly sources of energy such as wind, solar, wave and geothermal power.

Figure 4 Walking to school is better for the environment than going by car

Use less energy consuming devices. Encourage adults to address the problems.

Key ideas

★ Man and his activities have damaged the atmosphere
★ Carbon dioxide levels have increased in recent years
★ Green plants produce oxygen and remove carbon dioxide from the atmosphere
★ Removal of green plants changes the balance of oxygen and carbon dioxide in the atmosphere
★ Reduction in fossil fuel use is very important
★ The longer we wait before we take action the greater the environmental problems we will face

Wordbank

Atmosphere – gases that surround the Earth
Fossil fuels – coal, gas and oil
Photosynthesis – process carried out by green plants which removes carbon dioxide and adds oxygen to the atmosphere

Questions

1 What are the main gases found in the atmosphere?

2 Which gas found in the atmosphere is causing concern?

3 In what way do plants help animals?

4 Why will the removal of forests affect the levels of carbon dioxide in the atmosphere?

5 Why do industrialised countries produce more carbon dioxide?

6 Another name for global warming is the greenhouse effect. Why is this an appropriate name?

7 Select an environmentally friendly energy source and produce a report to explain why we should use it more.

8 Write a letter to your MP about your concerns for the environment.

9 Why should children be concerned about the environment?

39

Shula and Stuart were investigating how quickly sugar dissolved in water.

Shula said "I think it will dissolve faster if we use sugar cubes."

Stuart said "I think it will dissolve faster if we use the sugar grains."

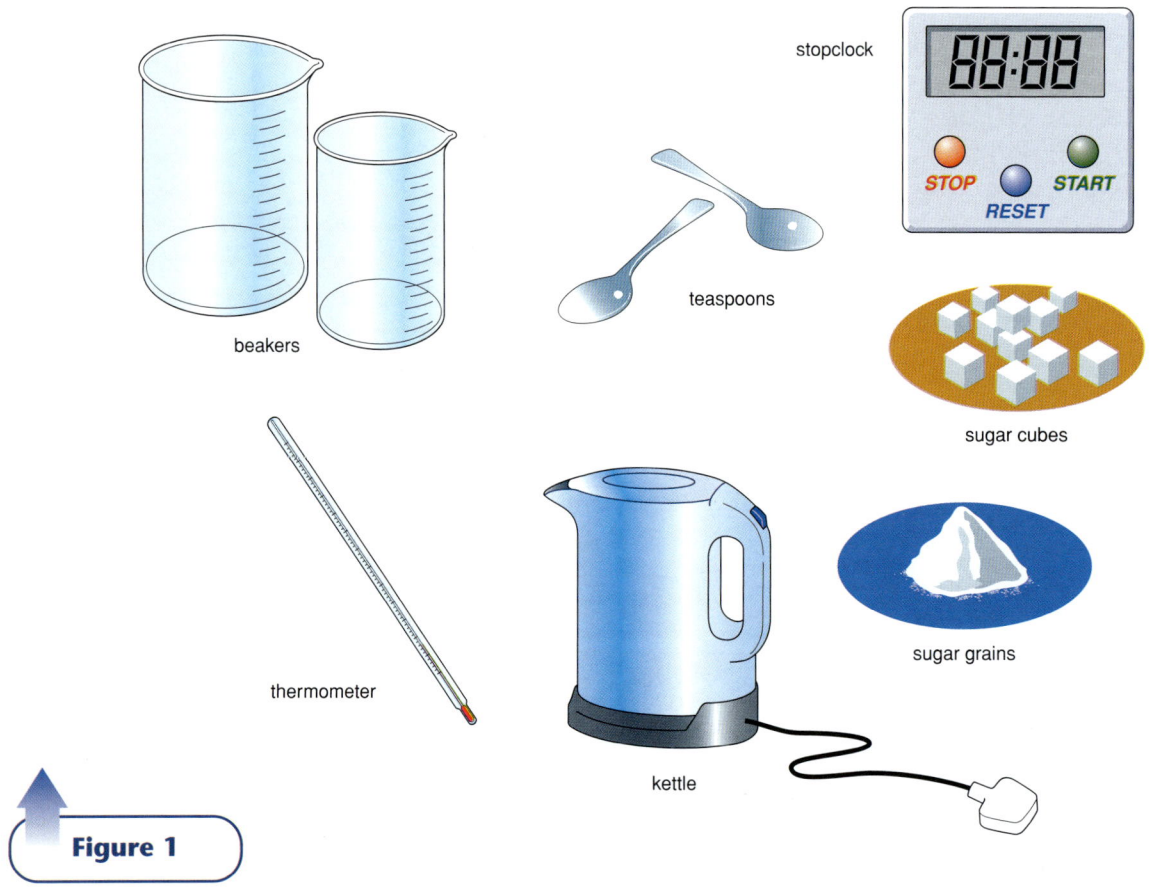

stopclock

teaspoons

sugar cubes

sugar grains

beakers

thermometer

kettle

Figure 1

Planning an investigation

Will the cubes of sugar or the grains of sugar dissolve more quickly? What do you think?

Plan an investigation to find out which prediction is correct.

Use these headings to help you.

1 What I want to find out.

2 The equipment I will need.

3 The way I will set it up.

4 What I will measure to find out who is correct.

5 What I predict will happen.

Fair testing

In order to get a good result, an investigation has to be a fair test. Figure 1 shows the equipment Shula and Stuart used to set up their investigation. Figure 2 shows how they carried out the investigation. Into a large beaker they added a teaspoon of sugar grains. Into a small beaker they added five cubes of sugar.

They used the spoon to stir the sugar from time to time.

Is this a fair test? Why do you think so?

Figure 2

Recording the results

Shula and Stuart changed the investigation so that it was a fair test. Then they did it three times and put their results in a table:

	Time taken		
	1st	2nd	3rd
Sugar grains	42 sec	51 sec	48 sec
Sugar cubes	1 min 49 sec	1 min 42 sec	1 min 54 sec

Table 1 Shula and Stuart's results

Questions

1 Why did they do the investigation three times?

2 Which dissolved faster – the sugar grains or the sugar cubes?

3 How do you know?

4 Why did one dissolve faster than the other?

Further Investigations

- Look back at the equipment that Shula and Stuart had at the start. They discovered that the size of the pieces of sugar made a difference to how quickly the sugar dissolved.

- What other variables might make a difference to the rate at which sugar dissolves?

- Choose one of the variables that you have thought of and make a prediction about how it will affect how quickly the sugar dissolves. Plan an investigation to find out if your prediction is correct.

Remember

- Investigations are about changing variables to see what happens as a result.

- Investigations are carried out to test predictions.

- Investigations must be fair tests.

- You must measure accurately and in the same way each time.

- You must record your findings – they are the evidence for your decisions.

Types of energy

Energy is found in different forms.

There are seven main forms of energy:

Heat energy

Sound energy

Electrical energy

Nuclear energy

Light energy

Movement energy

Stored energy

Each form of energy can be changed from one type into another.

Energy changes

On November 5 the family enjoy the fireworks display.

The burning bonfire changes **stored energy** from the wood into **heat energy** and **light energy**.

The rocket changes **stored energy** into **movement, sound** and **light energy**.

A nuclear power station changes **nuclear energy** into **electrical energy**. Electrical energy comes into your home and is changed into **light** and **heat energy** by the light bulb.

Key ideas

★ There are different forms of energy

★ These forms of energy can be changed from one form into another

Wordbank

Heat energy

Light energy

Sound energy

Movement energy

Electrical energy

Stored energy

Nuclear energy

Questions

1 Heat energy is produced by the cooker in your home. Suggest where in your home you would find the following types of energy:

a) light energy
b) sound energy
c) stored energy
d) movement energy.

2 Name four forms of energy you would expect to be produced by an automatic washing machine?

3 Your food contains stored energy. What forms of energy does your body change this stored energy into?

Throughout history we have used a variety of energy resources.

Stored energy in water

Coal

Oil

Nuclear

Wind

Wood

Gas

Solar

Geothermal

Non-renewable resources

Coal is a **fuel**. In the early 1900s coal was the main source of energy for industry and transport. Coal is a **non-renewable** energy resource. This means that some time in the future all of the coal will be burned. This fuel resource will be exhausted.

Other non-renewable energy resources include gas and oil. Coal, oil and gas are known as **fossil fuels**. They are formed from the bodies of dead animals and plants.

Renewable resources

Scientists are aware that fossil fuels are non-renewable and have for many years searched for energy resources which will not become exhausted. These are called **renewable** energy resources and include **solar**, wind, water and **geothermal**.

Solar energy

Solar energy is a relatively new source of energy in our homes and other buildings. Solar panels use the heat energy from the Sun to warm water for washing or for the central heating system. This form of energy produces very little **pollution** and so is growing in popularity.

Solar panels can also change light energy into electrical energy. The electrical energy produced by solar panels can be stored in **batteries** and used when it is dark at night.

Wind energy

The energy of the wind has been used for hundreds of years to turn windmills. Today, modern windmills are being built to convert wind energy into electricity. These windmills generate electricity without causing pollution but they can be noisy and spoil the quiet of the countryside.

Key ideas

- ★ There are many types of energy resources
- ★ Energy resources can be renewable or non-renewable
- ★ Solar energy comes from the Sun
- ★ Wind energy can be converted into electrical energy by modern windmills

Wordbank

Fuel – substance containing energy

Fossil fuel – coal, oil and gas

Solar – dependant upon the light energy from the Sun or other object

Geothermal – dependant upon the heat energy from the Earth

Batteries – special devices which can store electrical energy

Pollution – waste produced by humans which damages the environment

Questions

1 Name three non-renewable energy resources.

2 Name three renewable energy resources.

3 Explain why a forest could be described as a renewable energy resource.

4 Construct a question sheet for your class to find out the following information.

   a) What is the main energy resource used to heat your home?

   b) What is the main energy resource used to allow you to travel to school?

5 When you have collected all of your information for question 4, produce a bar chart for both a) and b).

Energy in the home

For any work to be done, there needs to be a source of energy.

A pot of water needs energy to make it boil.

A bulb needs energy to make it light.

A car needs energy to make it move along the road.

All of the energy that we need to make things work comes from a very small number of sources.

Chemical energy

Sometimes we use chemical energy to make things work. Chemical energy is stored in materials and it is released when, for example, the materials are burned. When gas is burned it gives out energy as heat. This makes the pot and the water warmer until the water boils.

Petrol gives out energy when it is put into the engine of a car. It is burned in very small amounts, very carefully, and the energy it gives out drives the motor and then the wheels.

We probably use **electrical energy** most in our houses.

Electrical energy

Electricity is used to do a lot of work in the home, at work and in school.

It can be used to heat things:

or to light a room:

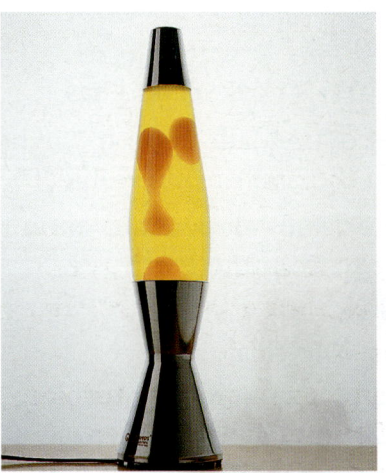

or to make a noise:

or to make things move:

Changing energy

The electrical energy is changed into other forms of energy – heat energy, light energy, sound or movement.

Each appliance uses electricity and changes it into a different form of energy.

In the electric fire, electricity is changed to heat energy.

In the lamp, electricity is changed into light energy.

In the radio, electricity is changed into sound energy.

In the fan, electricity is changed into movement energy.

When electricity is changed like this, scientists talk about it being **converted** into other forms of energy.

Key ideas

★ The energy we use comes from a range of sources

★ When we use a gas cooker or fire, we are using chemical energy

★ We use electrical energy to make many appliances in our homes work

★ Once inside our homes electricity is converted into different forms of energy

Wordbank

Energy source – the form of energy we use to make things work

Energy conversion – turning one form of energy into another

Questions

1 Name three energy sources we use in our homes or schools.

2 Complete these sentences:

   a) A washing machine turns electrical energy into _____ and _____.

   b) A radio turns electrical energy into _____ and _____.

   c) A television turns electrical energy into _____ and _____.

   d) A hairdryer turns electrical energy into _____ and _____.

3 Name a portable energy source and explain why it is useful to us.

Energy conversions involved in the generation of electricity

An energy conversion is when energy is changed from one form into another. The laws of science state that energy cannot be created nor destroyed. Energy can only be **transformed** from one form into another.

An example of this is when chemical energy in a gas cooker is changed into heat and light energy of the flame when the gas is burnt. We have not made nor destroyed the energy. We have changed it from chemical energy into heat and light energy.

Generating electricity

The most important source of energy that we use is electrical energy. We use electricity to heat and light our homes, as well as to run electrical appliances, such as hairdryers, televisions and washing machines. Electrical energy has to be produced from other forms of energy. We can transform a variety of energy types into electrical energy. To do this we need a special piece of apparatus called an electrical **generator**.

Power stations have enormous generators to produce all the electrical energy which we use in our homes and in industry. In an electrical generator, energy is fed into one end of a system and electrical energy is produced from the other.

Electricity from water

Figure 1 shows a **hydro-electric** power station. It produces electrical energy from the movement energy of falling water.

Electricity from fossil fuels

A lot of the electricity we use is generated by burning fuels, such as coal, oil and gas.

Figure 2 shows a gas powered generating system. Notice all the energy transformations which are involved.

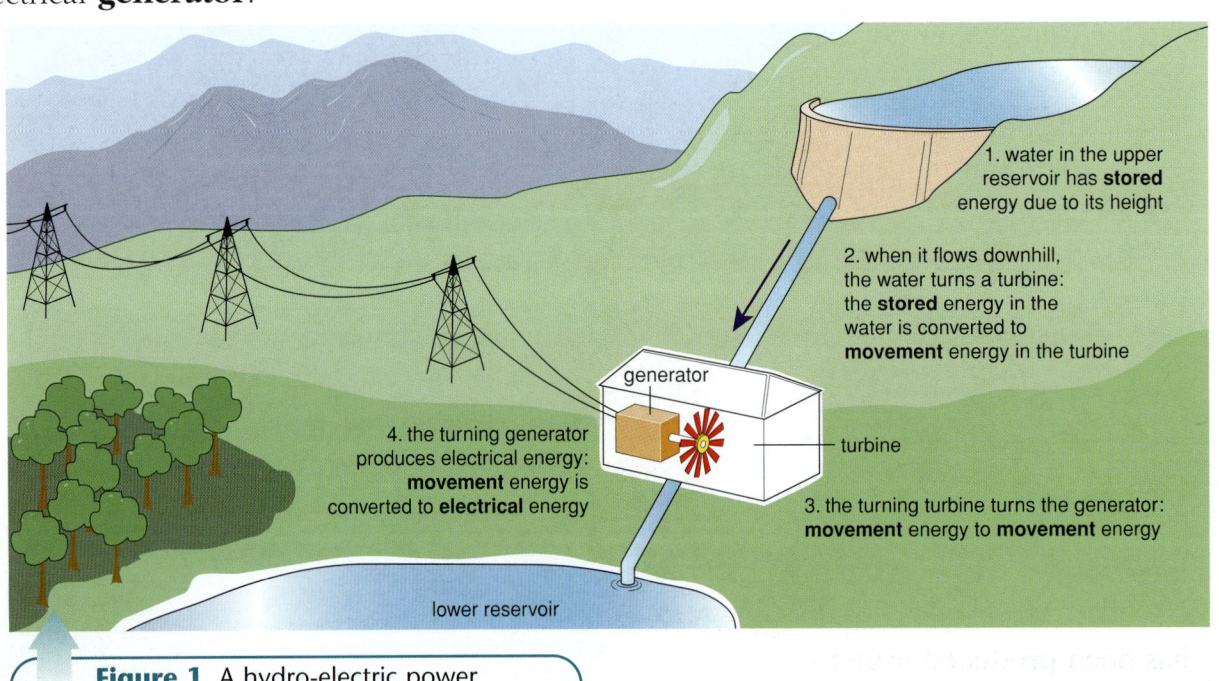

1. water in the upper reservoir has **stored** energy due to its height

2. when it flows downhill, the water turns a turbine: the **stored** energy in the water is converted to **movement** energy in the turbine

3. the turning turbine turns the generator: **movement** energy to **movement** energy

4. the turning generator produces electrical energy: **movement** energy is converted to **electrical** energy

generator

turbine

lower reservoir

Figure 1 A hydro-electric power station

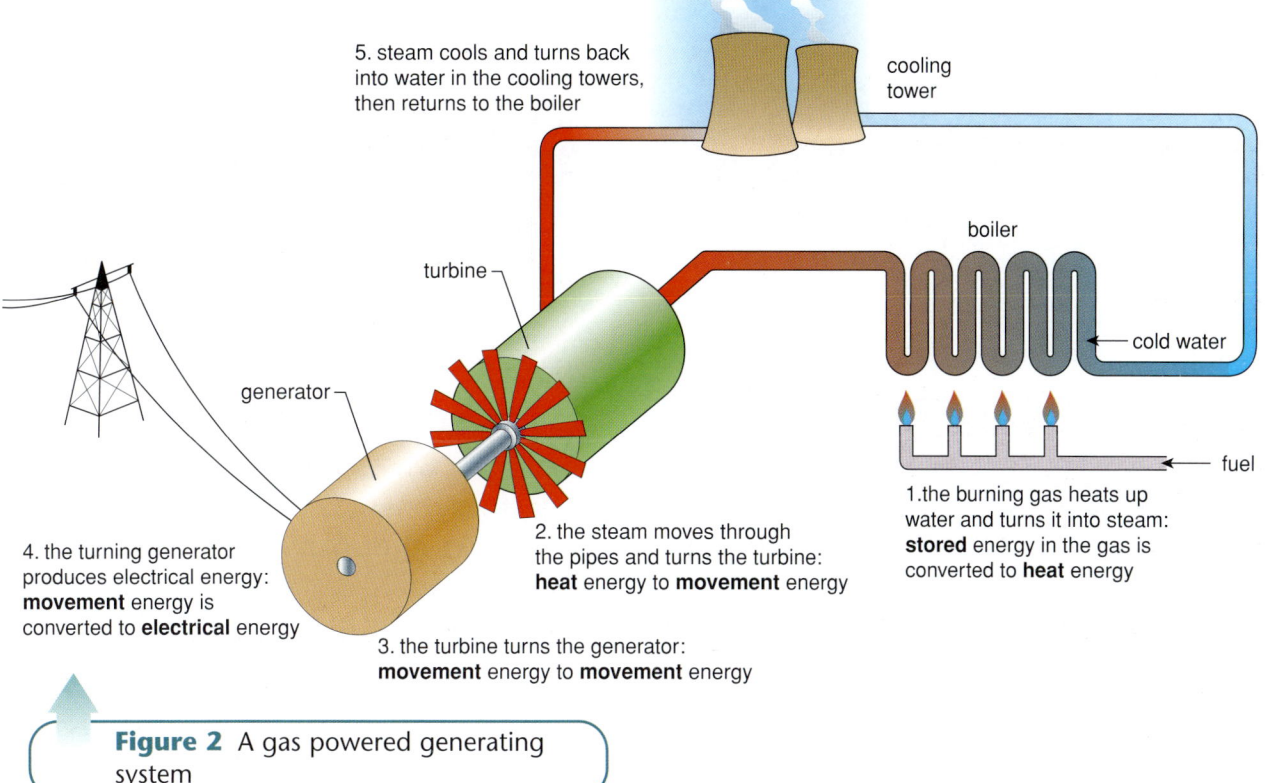

5. steam cools and turns back into water in the cooling towers, then returns to the boiler

cooling tower

boiler

cold water

turbine

generator

fuel

1.the burning gas heats up water and turns it into steam: **stored** energy in the gas is converted to **heat** energy

4. the turning generator produces electrical energy: **movement** energy is converted to **electrical** energy

2. the steam moves through the pipes and turns the turbine: **heat** energy to **movement** energy

3. the turbine turns the generator: **movement** energy to **movement** energy

Figure 2 A gas powered generating system

The electricity produced by power stations then travels along power lines to be used in our homes and in industry.

The network of cables that covers the country is called the **National Grid**.

Key ideas

★ A power station converts energy from one form into another

★ Different types of power station use different types of energy resources

★ The generator is the piece of apparatus which produces the electrical energy

Wordbank

Transform – to change from one form into another

Generator – piece of apparatus which changes movement energy into electrical energy

Hydro-electric – electrical energy which has been produced from the movement energy of falling water

Questions

1 Rearrange the following forms of energy in the order they would be found, from the boiler to the power lines in a gas power station?

electrical energy
movement energy
heat energy
movement energy
stored energy

2 Suggest two types of power station not mentioned in the passage.

3 Find out where the nearest power station is to you. How does this power station produce electrical energy?

The electrical energy produced by generators in power station has to be distributed to all the homes, offices, shops and industries which wish to use it. This requires a very complicated network of electricity-carrying cables called the **National Grid**. You can see the cables carried by pylons across the country.

Figure 1 Many people think that the pylons are an eye-sore. What do you think?

There are many different power stations around the country each of which generate electrical energy and pass it into the National Grid.

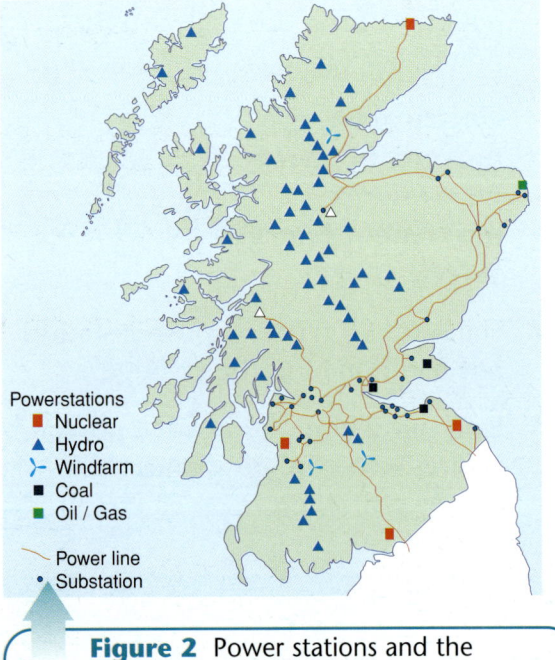

Powerstations
- Nuclear
- Hydro
- Windfarm
- Coal
- Oil / Gas

— Power line
· Substation

Figure 2 Power stations and the National Grid in Scotland

In Scotland the main producers of electricity are called *Scottish Power* and *Scottish Hydro Electric*. These companies are responsible for generating and supplying electrical energy to the whole of Scotland.

Getting connected

The complex network of cables starts off at generators, which produce huge amounts of electrical energy. The electrical energy flows along **aluminium** wires that hang from the pylons. Aluminium is a very good conductor of electricity.

The pylons hold the aluminium cables high above the ground. This is because the voltage is so large that it is very dangerous to humans.

Safe height 16'-6"

Figure 3 You must be careful if there are overhead electricity cables

Electricity companies have to change the flow of electricity so that it is not dangerous to people. They do this with special devices called **transformers**.

When the overhead cables reach a town or city the cables are connected to a substation containing a transformer which decreases the voltage.

Figure 4 At this substation the voltage is reduced to make it safer

The electricity is then fed to another substation normally close to where the electricity is needed. Here the voltage is decreased again and sent to the homes, offices, shops and industries where it is needed.

All of the steps in this process are controlled by the electricity companies.

Straight to you

Electricity comes into your house through cables. In each house there is an electricity meter that measures how much electrical energy you use. Then the electricity company knows how much to charge you for the electrical energy you use.

Figure 5 Electricity meter in house

Do you know where the electricity meter is in your home? If you do not, try to find out.

Key ideas

★ The National Grid is a system which allows electricity to be distributed around the country

★ High voltage is dangerous to humans

★ Transformers are used to change the voltage to make it safer near town and cities

Questions

1 Where is electricity produced?

2 What metal is used to make the cables, which carry the electricity in the National Grid?

3 Which power company produces the electricity used in your school?

4 How does the electricity get into your house?

5 Why do you have an electricity meter in your house?

Wordbank

National Grid – the network of electricity carrying cables

Transformer – electrical device which can change the voltage either up or down

Aluminium – metal used to make National Grid cables

In our homes we use electricity to make lots of appliances work: kettles, washing machines, cookers and fridges all use electricity.

They have cables attached to them and they are plugged into the mains electricity that comes to our homes through the **National Grid**.

Not all of the electricity we use comes from the National Grid. We also use electricity to make small appliances work – like torches, personal stereos and cameras.

Figure 1 All these appliances use electricity

Where does the electricity come from to work these appliances?

If you take a torch apart, you can see that it made up of a battery, a bulb and some metal strips. The case around the outside holds it all together.

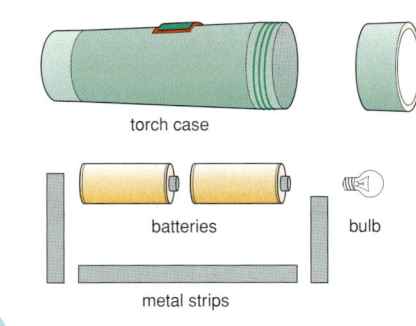

torch case

batteries

bulb

metal strips

Figure 2 What you would find if you took a torch apart

The battery provides a source of electrical energy for the torch. The electrical energy is converted into light energy when it reaches the bulb.

The bulb will only light if there is a path for the electrical energy to travel from the battery to the bulb. The metal wires provide this path, connecting the battery and the bulb together. Metal wires are used because metals are usually better than any other material for carrying or **conducting** electricity. This is called an **electrical circuit**.

The bulb has two places for connecting it in a circuit, called **terminals**. The battery has two terminals as well.

The terminals need to be connected in a particular way to form an electrical circuit.

Here the bulb is connected to the battery in a circuit. The bulb is lit up.

Figure 3 The bulb lights up because there is a path for the electrical energy

If the circuit had any gaps in it at all, the electrical energy would not be able to travel from the battery to the bulb and it would not light. A circuit which has no gaps is called a **closed circuit**.

If there is a gap in a circuit and the electrical energy cannot flow through it, it is called an **open circuit**.

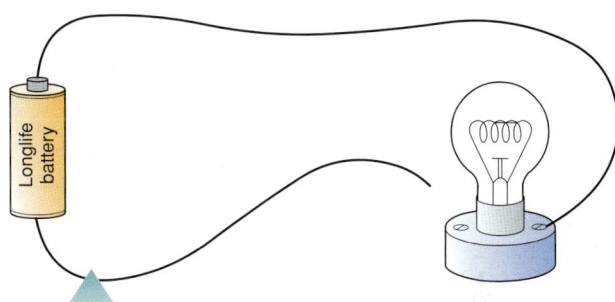

Figure 4 The bulb is not lit up because there is no path for the electrical energy

Key ideas

★ Electrical circuits are pathways which carry electrical energy

★ Metal wires are used in electrical circuits because metal is usually better than any other material for **conducting** electricity

★ A battery has to be connected in a particular way to form a circuit

★ Circuits may be open or closed. Open circuits cannot conduct electrical energy

Wordbank

Conductor – material which carries electricity e.g. metal wire

Electrical circuit – path of electricity connected to a source of electricity

Closed circuit – circuit with no gaps so electricity can flow round it

Open circuit – circuit which has gaps and that electricity cannot flow around

Questions

1 How does a torch work?

2 In a torch, what form of energy is the electricity converted into?

3 Will a torch work without a battery? Why do you think so?

4 Look at each of these circuits and say whether it is **open** or **closed**.

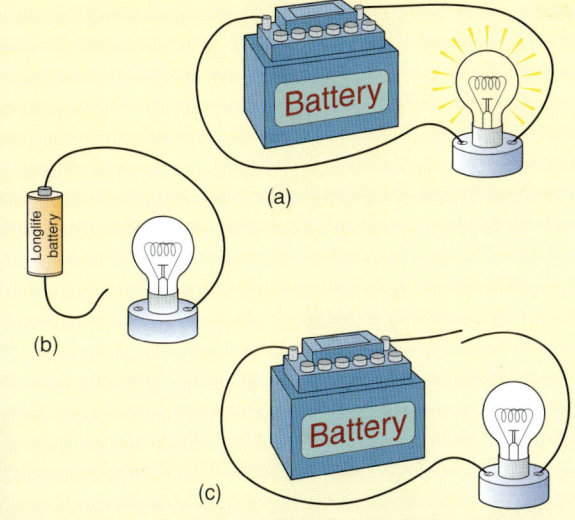

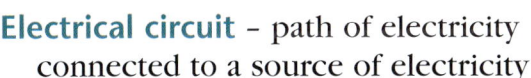

(a)

(b)

(c)

53

We can connect a battery and bulb together with metal wires to make the bulb light up.

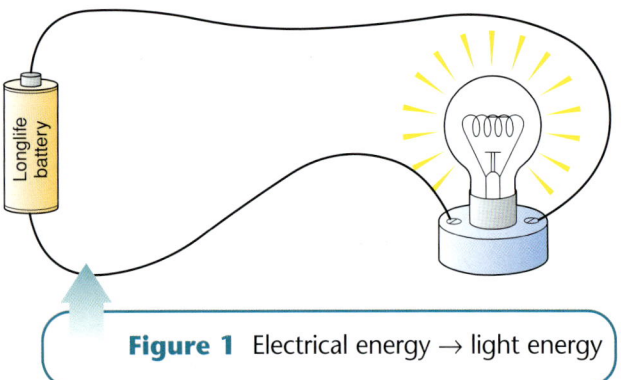

Figure 1 Electrical energy → light energy

Instead of a bulb, we could put a buzzer in the circuit. The electricity would then be converted into sound energy instead of light energy.

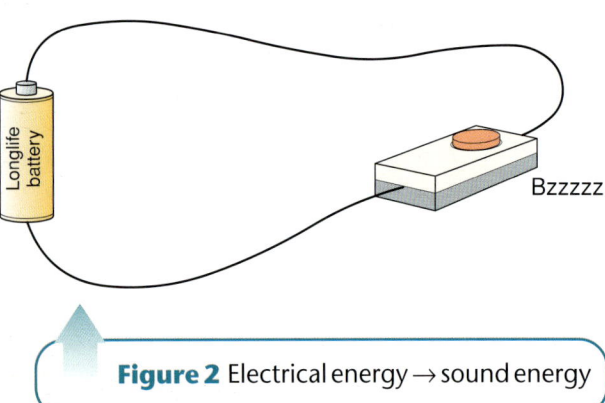

Bzzzzz

Figure 2 Electrical energy → sound energy

We do not usually want a bulb or a buzzer to be on all of the time. If we add another **electrical component**, a **switch**, to the circuit, we will be able to do this. Here are some simple switches.

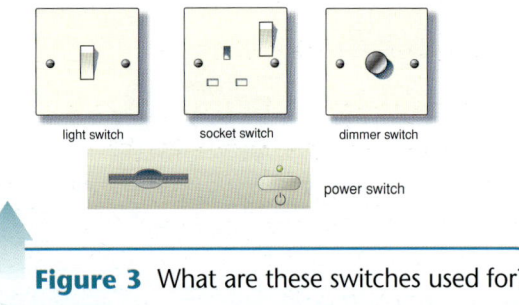

light switch   socket switch   dimmer switch

power switch

Figure 3 What are these switches used for?

Switches are made so that they can be open or closed. This switch is open and the electricity cannot flow through the gap.

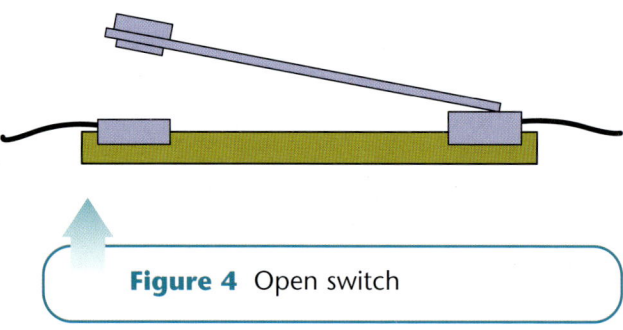

Figure 4 Open switch

When you press down on the switch, it closes and the electricity can flow through the circuit again.

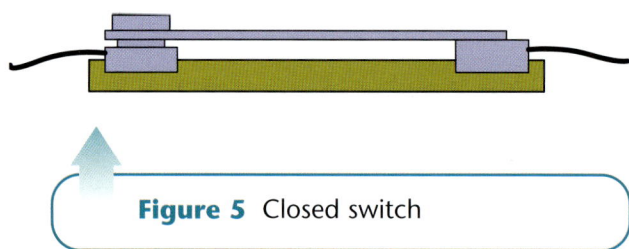

Figure 5 Closed switch

The switch goes into the circuit like this:

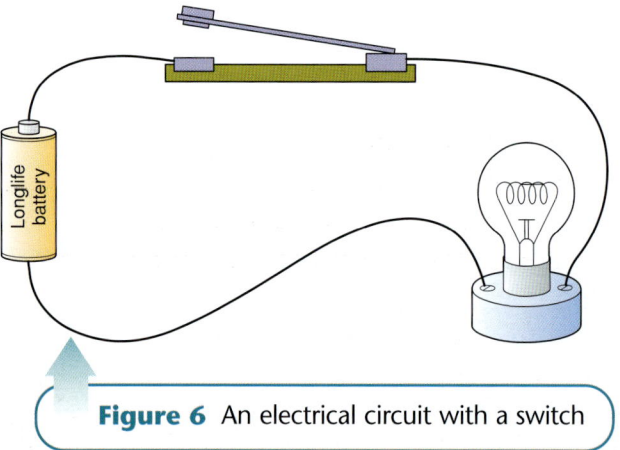

Figure 6 An electrical circuit with a switch

In a circuit like this, the electricity cannot flow until the switch is closed. Pressing down on the switch will close the circuit and the bulb will light. The switches that you use in torches and lamps are made like this – but you do not have to press down on them to keep them switched on!

When we put electrical components together in a circuit like this, it is called a **series circuit**.

In a series circuit, all of the components form a single path around the circuit – the arrows in this drawing show you the path that the electrical energy takes from the battery, through the switch and the buzzer and back to the battery.

It does not matter if we put the switch before or after the bulb; the bulb will only light when the switch is closed, forming a closed circuit.

A series circuit can have several electrical components but they all must be connected to make a single path for the electrical energy.

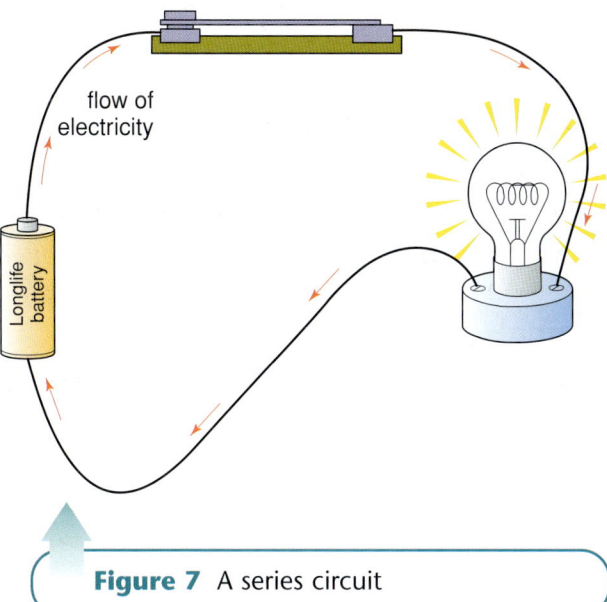

flow of electricity

Longlife battery

Figure 7 A series circuit

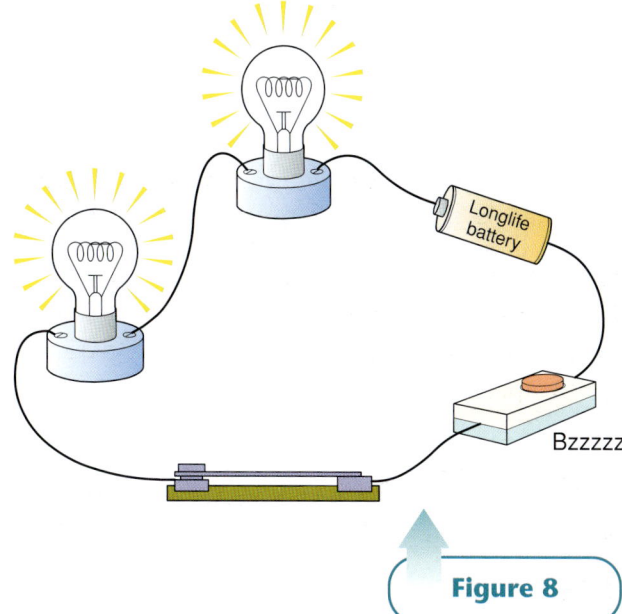

Longlife battery

Bzzzzz

Figure 8

Key ideas

★ Electrical energy will only flow around a closed circuit
★ A switch can be used to control the flow of electricity around a circuit

Wordbank

Electrical component - part of an electrical circuit

Switch - a component which can be used to change a circuit from open to closed and so control the flow of electricity around a circuit

Series circuit - a circuit which has a single pathway for the electricity

Questions

1 A bulb is an electrical component. Name two other electrical components.

2 When the switch is open, the bulb will not light. Why?

3 Why do we need switches in electrical circuits?

4 What is a **serie**s circuit?

5 Draw a circuit that has a battery, a switch and two bulbs in series.

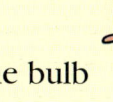

28

Symbols and Diagrams

When people draw electrical components and circuits, it is sometimes difficult to tell what it is they have drawn. Some components are difficult to draw and so, instead of making a drawing of a component, we use a symbol to represent each component.

Here are some of the common **electrical symbols** that are used:

Component	Symbol	What it does
bulb		converts electrical energy to light energy
battery		a store of electrical energy
switch		used to open and close a circuit
buzzer		converts electrical energy to sound energy
motor		converts electrical energy to movement energy

Table 1 Symbols for electrical components

When electrical components are together in a circuit, they are put together in a **circuit diagram**. Here is a circuit diagram of a simple circuit with a bulb and a battery:

The wires in a circuit are always drawn as straight lines, with sharp corners.

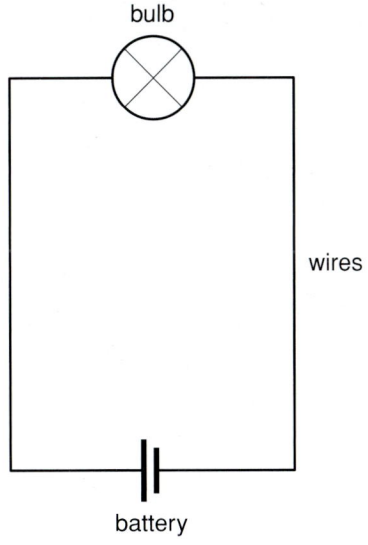

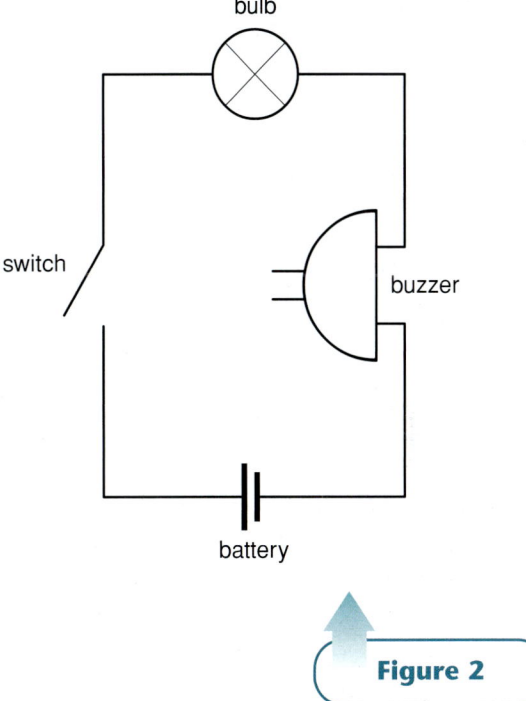

Figure 1 A simple circuit diagram

Figure 2

Here is a circuit diagram for a more complicated circuit.

Key ideas

★ Symbols are used to represent the components in electrical circuits

★ Circuit diagrams are used to represent electrical circuits

Wordbank

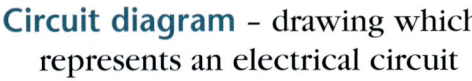

Electrical symbols – symbols which represent electrical components

Circuit diagram – drawing which represents an electrical circuit

Questions

1 Why do we use symbols to show electrical circuits rather than drawings?

2 Draw a diagram for a series circuit that contains one bulb, a buzzer, a battery and a switch.

3 Make a circuit then draw the diagram. See if someone else can make the same circuit from your drawing.

29

Simple lenses and how they work

Lens (lenz) *n*! a piece of glass or other transparent material used to converge or diverge transmitted light and form optical images.

Optical images – the pictures that are made by the lenses e.g. what you see through binoculars or a microscope.

Transparent – it is essential that light passes through lenses. Dirt can stop lenses working properly. Sometimes they are coloured e.g. sunglasses.

Glass – is a useful material for making lenses. The first telescope was perfected by Galileo in the 17th century. He brought glass lenses from Holland to Italy.

Converge – some lenses can focus light on a point.

Diverge – other lenses can spread light apart.

Material – modern lenses are made of plastics.

Figure 1 Lenses and their properties

What lenses do

Lenses bend light. In other words light changes direction when it passes through a lens. Window glass is flat and does not bend light. Although the glass is transparent, it is flat and light passes through without being bent. Lenses are made from shaped glass (or plastic) and there are two main types – **concave** and **convex**.

Concave lenses

Concave lenses bend light outwards. They cause the light rays to spread apart or **diverge**.

(Here is how to remember their shape – concave – they go inwards like a cave.)

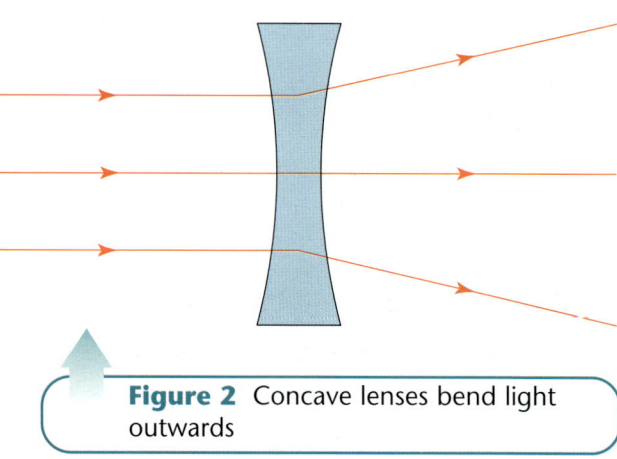

Figure 2 Concave lenses bend light outwards

Convex lenses

Convex lenses bend light inwards so that it can be focused on a single point. The light rays are said to **converge**.

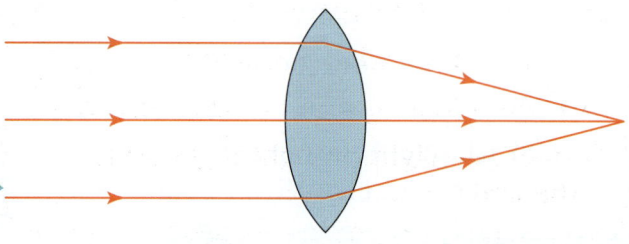

Figure 3 Convex lenses bend light inwards

Each of our eyes contains a convex lens. The lens helps us to focus light so that we can see clearly.

You might have used a lens to focus the light of the sun and burn a piece of paper.

Figure 4 Peter is using a lens to focus the light of the Sun. Poor Sophie!

Here is a simple lens

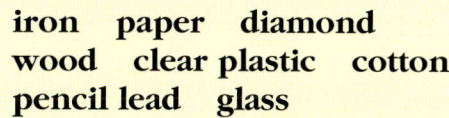

Figure 5 Water is a simple lens!

The water acts as a lens because it is transparent and is shaped. This allows it to bend the light. In Figure 5, the water magnifies the cat's face.

Key ideas

★ Lenses are transparent and have a shape
★ Lenses can be made from any transparent, shaped material
★ Lenses bend light
★ Convex lenses bend light inwards
★ Concave lenses bend light outwards

Wordbank

Lens – transparent material that is shaped so that it may bend light

Concave – a lens that is shaped ⧗

Convex – a lens that is shaped ()

Diverge – light spread out from the lens

Converge – light brought together from the lens

Questions

1 Which of the following materials could be used to make a lens?

   iron   paper   diamond wood   clear plastic   cotton pencil lead   glass

2 What needs to be done to each of the materials before they can be used as a lens?

3 Use some of the following words to complete the sentences:

   concave   convex   spreads focus   inwards   outwards

   A <u>concave</u> lens bends the light _____.

   A _____ lens bends the light _____.

4 Explain why water can be used as a lens.

30

The application of lenses

Lenses may be made from many materials – glass and plastic are the most popular. Lenses are used to look at very small things, which we cannot see with our eyes. They are also used to study things which are very far away.

Lenses can be used to look at very small things

The simplest is a hand lens. Hold the hand lens close to your eye and then focus on the object that you are observing by moving it closer to the lens. The lens **magnifies** the object – makes it look bigger.

Figure 1 Using a hand lens

Microscopes contain lenses.

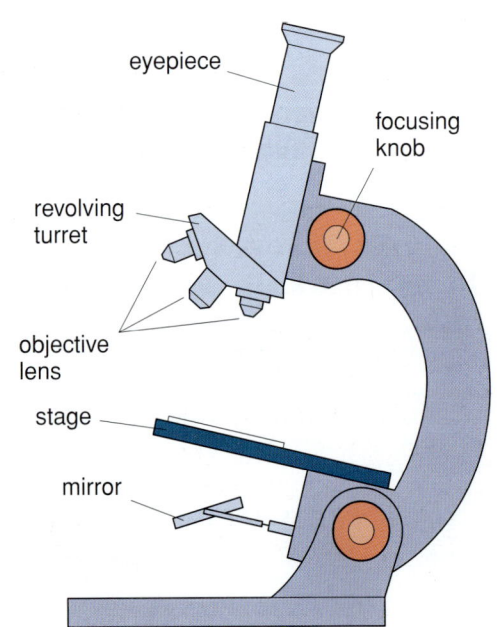

eyepiece

focusing knob

revolving turret

objective lens

stage

mirror

This type of microscope contains more than one lens. The image is magnified by the first lens and is then further magnified by a second lens. The microscope's maximum magnification should be about times 1000.

Microscopes like this are used by scientists, for example to examine bacteria, crystals in rock and to count blood cells.

Lenses are used to make things appear bigger

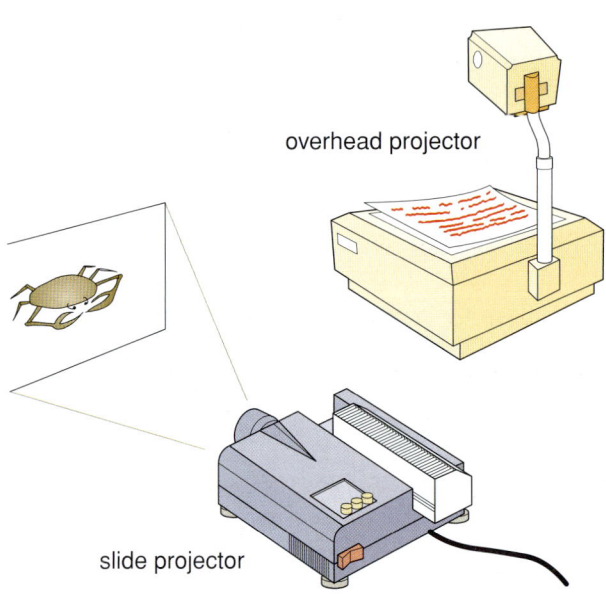

overhead projector

slide projector

The lenses in the overhead projector in the classroom and the slide projector can make small pictures appear much bigger. This allows many people to see them.

Lenses are also used in the film projector at the cinema. One problem is that the light behind the lenses must be very bright and the projector can become very hot. Another problem is that the room has to be dark so that everyone may see.

Figure 2 A microscope

Lenses are used to look at things that are far away

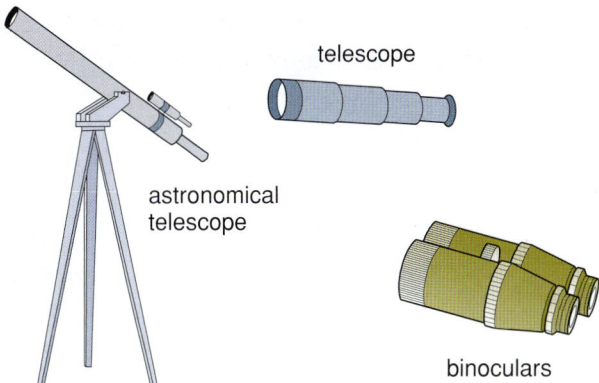

telescope

astronomical telescope

binoculars

In 1609, **Galileo** – an Italian scientist – heard about a "spyglass" that a Dutchman had brought to Venice. Rumour had it that this spyglass could be used to see the stars.

Galileo made his own **telescope** and went on to make discoveries about the Moon, the stars and the Solar System. Other people then used the telescope at sea and on land for navigation. Sometimes they even used it for spying on other people!

Binoculars are like two telescopes stuck together so that you can use both eyes to look at objects that are far away. It is funny to think that telescopes and binoculars both work in the same way as a microscope – the image magnified by one lens can be further magnified by another.

Lenses correct our vision

Some people have got 'specs appeal'! Sometimes the lens inside the eye or other parts of the eye prevents people from seeing properly. The two main problems – short sight and long sight – are both corrected by wearing glasses.

Key ideas

★ Lenses have many applications

★ Lenses are used to
- look at very small things
- look at things that are far away
- make things appear bigger
- correct our vision

Wordbank

Magnify – to make things look bigger

Microscope – instrument used to see small things

Galileo – a famous Italian scientist

Telescope/Binoculars – instruments used to see distant objects

Questions

1 Describe the best way to use a hand lens.

2 Did Galileo invent the telescope?

3 Look up the word 'binocular' in the dictionary. What does it mean?

4 What two problems exist when lenses are used to make pictures bigger in projectors?

5 If you were to invent a new material for making lenses what would be the two most important properties?

6 Make a table to show the four main applications of lenses and give examples of each.

Application	Example
1 to look at very small things	
2	
3	
4	

When you buy an ice cream, you expect it to be cold. When you buy a cup of coffee, you expect it to be hot.

On summer days, you expect it to be hotter than on winter days.

Which things in this picture would you expect to be hot and which would you expect to be cold? Why?

Heat energy

Heat is a form of energy. Things are hot or cold because of how much heat energy they have. When we give heat energy to something, it can change.

The heat energy from the sun melts the snow.

The heat energy from the flame cooks the egg.

The heat energy from the fire burns the wood, giving off flames and smoke.

Measuring temperature

We use a **thermometer** to tell how hot or cold something is by measuring its **temperature**. When we measure temperature, we get an idea of how much heat energy it has. There are different kinds of thermometers for different purposes.

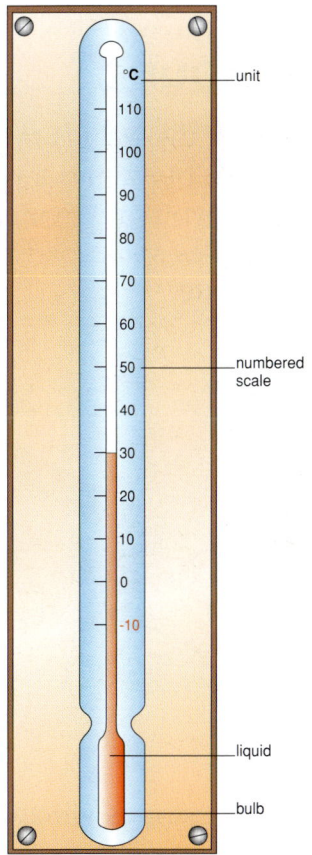

Figure 1 A thermometer

We measure temperature in units called degrees **Celsius** – written like this: 8 C. You can see the temperature scale along the side of the thermometer.

You might use a digital thermometer in your classroom. A digital thermometer shows the temperature in numbers, rather like a digital watch.

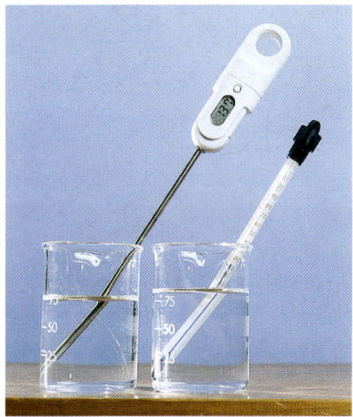

Figure 2 Thermometers

Key ideas

★ Heat is a form of energy
★ Temperature is a measure of how much heat energy something has
★ We measure temperature using a thermometer in degrees Celsius (8 C)

Wordbank

Temperature – a measure of how hot or cold something is

Thermometer – the instrument used to measure temperature

Celsius – the scale we use to measure temperature

Questions

1 What do we use to measure temperature?

2 Here is a list of the temperature in Europe on 28th December.

City	Temperature (8 C)	Weather
Amsterdam	2 1	Snow
Berlin	1	Drizzle
Dublin	0	Sunny
Geneva	6	Cloudy
Glasgow	2 4	Mist
London	2	Dull
Rome	16	Rain

   a) Which city was the coldest?
   b) Which one was the warmest?

3 Read the temperatures on these three thermometers:

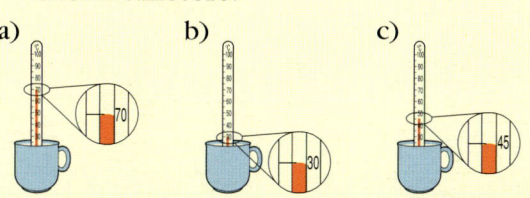

a)   b)   c)

Making noise

Do you like listening to music? Here are some musical instruments that make quite different sounds. Each sound is made in a different way.

A guitar makes a sound when the strings are plucked.

A drum makes a sound when you hit it with a drumstick.

A trumpet makes a sound when you blow into it.

What is sound?

When you pluck the strings of a guitar, bang on a drum, blow into a trumpet or strike a triangle, you are giving out energy. That energy makes some part of the instrument **vibrate**.

In the guitar, the strings vibrate.

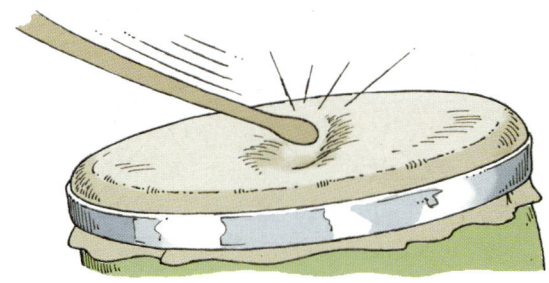

In the drum, the skin of the drum vibrates.

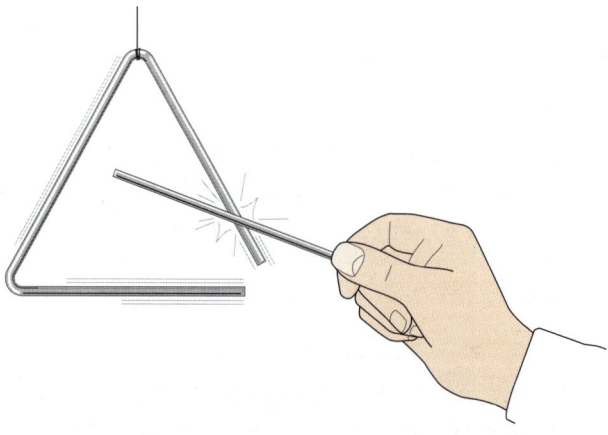

In a triangle, it is the metal that vibrates.

The vibrations make the air round about the instrument vibrate too. The vibrations made by the guitar strings, drum skin and triangle make the air vibrate.

When these vibrations reach our ears, we hear them as sounds.

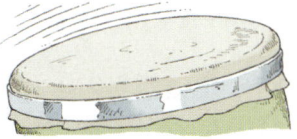

Figure 1 The drum skin makes the air around it vibrate

Figure 2 When vibrations from the musical instruments reach the conductor, he hears them as sounds

Key ideas

★ Sound is a form of energy
★ We hear sounds because the energy makes the air vibrate and the vibrations reach our ears

Wordbank

Vibrations – the way something (a string, drum skin or the air) moves backwards and forwards

Questions

1 How are sounds made?
2 Copy this table and complete it.

Instrument	Sound is made by
Drum	striking its surface
Violin	
Tambourine	
Flute	
Saxophone	
Piano	

33 Volume and pitch

Sounds can be soft or loud depending how close to the source of the noise you are.

Figure 1 Sounds are different depending on how close or far you are from the source of the sounds

You can make the sound of a drum louder by striking it harder. In that way you give it more energy and the vibrations are bigger. If you strike it very gently, you give it only a little energy and you get small vibrations and a very quiet sound. The loudness of a sound is called its **volume**.

a)

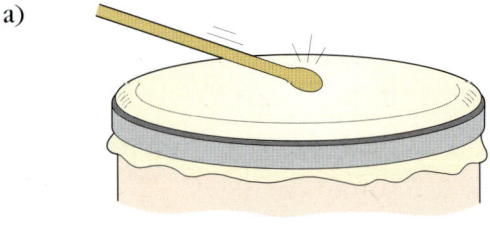

b)

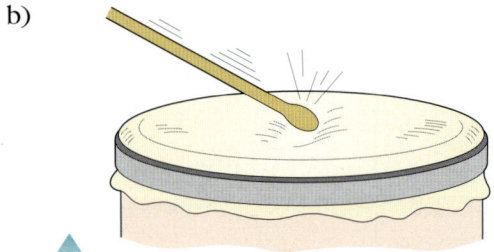

Figure 2 Sounds of different volume can be produced when this drum is hit a) gently or b) hard

Sounds can be high or low. A big drum makes a big, deep sound; a small drum makes a much higher sound. It does not matter how hard you hit it.

The thick strings on a guitar make a low sound but the thin strings sound much higher. This is the **pitch** of a sound (how high or low it is).

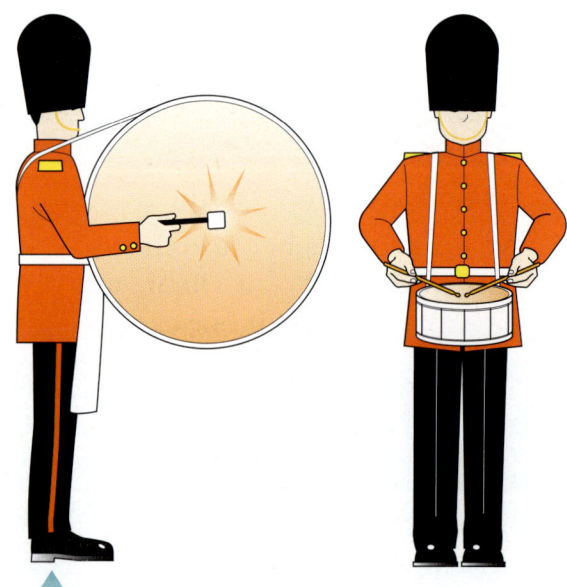

Figure 3 A big drum makes a sound with a lower pitch than a small drum

Figure 4 The thick strings on a guitar have a low pitch

The pitch of a sound depends on how quickly the vibrations move through the air. A small instrument vibrates very quickly (a small drum or a thin guitar string). A big instrument vibrates very slowly and gives a low note. It has a low pitch.

Every sound has both **pitch** and **volume**.

For example a mouse's squeak has a high pitch and a low volume.

An elephant makes a sound that has a low pitch but a high volume.

Key ideas

★ Sounds have both pitch and volume

★ Volume is increased by using more energy

★ The pitch of a sound depends on how fast the instrument is vibrating

Wordbank

Volume – how loud or quiet a sound is

Pitch – how low or high the sound is

Questions

1 What is the difference between volume and pitch?

2 Which of these two singers will have the highest pitch: a soprano or a tenor?

3 Identify the volume and pitch for each of these everyday noises. The first one is done for you.

Noise	Volume Loud	Volume Quiet	Pitch High	Pitch Low
Ambulance siren	✓		✓	
Thunder				
Bicycle bell				
Telephone				
Door bell				
Car engine				
Bird song				
Kettle boiling				

Slow down – You'll cause friction!

How do cars and buses slow down? Why are cars more likely to skid on a wet road than they are on a dry road?

The answer is because of **friction**.

What is friction?

Friction is the name we give to the force involved when objects rub together.

It is friction that makes it difficult for us to push large objects across the floor.

Friction is a force that slows us down and helps us stop.

Friction occurs when surfaces rub against each other and when this happens it can wear away the surfaces.

Figure 1 Friction has worn away these surfaces

Friction is involved in our everyday life and we are used to dealing with it, but many people think that friction only occurs when solid objects come into contact. Friction occurs in **every** type of substance.

Friction in liquids

It is more difficult for us to walk through a deep stream than it is to walk through air.

Figure 2 This tanker is being pushed through the water by two tugboats

This is because the water rubs against our legs and causes friction. If we try to move our legs quickly we find that it becomes very difficult and very tiring!

People swim when in water not only because its fun but because it can be a better method of pushing through the water when it is deep.

Friction in gases

Figure 3 These people are experiencing friction!

Although there is less friction in gases and we tend not to think about it too much, it can still have an effect on us. Take a sheet of paper and let it fall to the ground.

Now crumple it up and drop it.

Air friction slows the open sheet down so it drops much slower than the crumpled sheet.

Parachutes use air friction to stop us from flying through the air too quickly.

What does friction do?

Friction occurs when different objects come into contact with each other.

The first thing it does is to make it more difficult for the objects to move. It generally slows them down.

Car tyres rubbing against tarmac roads cause a lot of friction and this helps slow the car down.

It can also cause a lot of heat. If you take a block of wood and rub it hard along the pavement it will get warm.

People rub their hands together in order to get their fingers warm. The friction caused by rubbing creates heat and this warms your fingers.

Key ideas

★ Friction is a force that slows us down

★ Friction occurs when different objects rub against each other

★ Friction can cause objects to be worn down

★ Friction can cause heat to be produced

Wordbank

Friction – the force of resistance working against movement

Questions

1 How do brakes on your bike slow you down?

2 Why do you slide if you run in the gym with only your socks on your feet?

3 Why would it be difficult to play football on ice?

4 Why do people put wheels on the bottom of heavy pieces of furniture?

5 What could you do to make your shoes have less grip? (*Hint*: reduce friction.)

35

Reducing friction – Streamlining in animals

Friction is a force that slows us down but sometimes we do not want to be slowed down.

If we want to travel quickly or easily through air or water it would help us if we could reduce the friction that causes us to slow down.

This can be done by making a shape that is easier to push through air or water.

This is called **streamlining**.

Streamlining means to make a shape that can push through air or water easily.

Look at the shapes of the following animals and think which ones are able to move rapidly.

Some of these animals have developed so that they can move quickly. Their shapes make it easier for them to cut through the air or water and this has helped them survive over the years.

Why are their shapes streamlined?

Certain shapes can slide through air and water quite easily.

The air can slide over them without causing much air resistance.

Smooth, rounded shapes can pass through without a great deal of friction or air resistance.

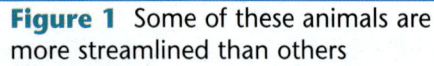
Figure 1 Some of these animals are more streamlined than others

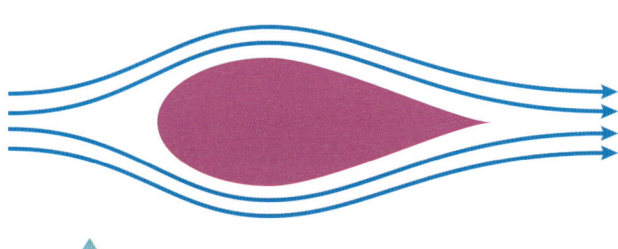
Figure 2 A smooth, rounded shape lets air flow round it

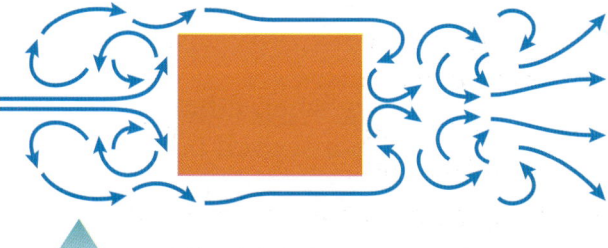
Figure 3 A large, square shape stops the flow of air – friction

Large, square shapes have to push a lot of air out of the way and this makes it difficult for those shapes to pass easily.

Any animal that wants to move quickly would do better if it had a rounded shape that tailed off smoothly.

Look at these streamlined animals.

a)

b)

c)

Figure 4
a) A dolphin b) a shark c) a gannet

How can we travel more quickly?

Have a look at a swimming competition. All the swimmers wear a cap or shave their heads to make themselves more streamlined. Many male swimmers have been known to shave off all the hair on their chest, arms and legs as well!

Cyclists also shave the hair on their legs. In addition to this they wear tight fitting clothes made of smooth material that help them cut through the air.

Depending on the event, some wear a funny shaped helmet which cuts down the air resistance.

Figure 5 An Olympic cyclist

Key ideas

★ Certain shapes can reduce air friction and air resistance

★ Smooth rounded shapes are the most streamlined

★ Many animals have evolved into a streamlined shape naturally

★ People can do things which will make them more streamlined

Wordbank

Streamlined – a shape which reduces friction

Questions

1 List five animals that have a streamlined shape.

2 Draw the seal and show how the water would flow over it when it was swimming.

3 What do swimmers do to make themselves more streamlined?

4 Draw the cyclist in Figure 5 and show the air flowing over him.

36

Reducing friction – Streamlining in cars, trains, boats and planes

We saw in the last chapter how certain animals have evolved **streamlined** shapes. By being streamlined animals reduce friction and therefore use less energy to move. We can use the same ideas to make it easier for us to move things.

The shape of cars, lorries and trains can be altered so that they can travel through the air more smoothly.

Compare the shapes of these 'older' cars and lorries with more recent models.

Figure 1 Which of these is more streamlined?

You can see how some shapes are more streamlined. This means that these vehicles can move more quickly and go faster without using as much fuel.

If a vehicle wants to go *very* quickly it helps if we make it even more streamlined. Look at this racing car.

Figure 2 A Formula 1 racing car

The streamlined shape really only helps when the vehicle is travelling at a high speed. Making a double decker bus more streamlined would only make a tiny difference to its performance as it is meant to go slowly and stop a lot of the time.

Trains, boats and planes

Streamlined shapes are used to improve the performance of not only cars, but many other fast moving objects today. The shape of local trains is fairly square but high speed trains have a smooth, rounded front so that they can travel smoothly at speeds greater than 100 miles an hour.

Figure 3 This high speed train is used in Japan

Many boats are streamlined. They are streamlined above and below the water line. This is because they have to push through water and air.

Water is more dense than air. More friction is produced by an object moving through water than through air. Therefore it takes more energy to move through water. Because of this many modern boats have an additional feature that helps them travel more easily.

Figure 4 This boat pushes itself out of the water

When they start to move quickly, the water pushes the boat upwards so that less of the boat is in contact with the water. This means that more of the boat is pushing through air – letting the boat move more easily.

The fastest moving things today are aeroplanes. Normal passenger planes fly at about 500 mph while fighter jets can fly at more than 1000 mph.

When objects are travelling at this speed they need to be very streamlined. A flat square shape would cause the 'planes to slow down very quickly. In fact aeroplanes have parts of the wings which are meant to do that. They help slow down the aeroplane prior to landing.

All aeroplanes have smooth, rounded noses which reduce air friction.

Figure 5 This stealth plane is very streamlined and travels faster than passenger aeroplanes

Key ideas

★ Streamlining is used to improve the way many vehicles move

★ Modern vehicles have similar rounded shapes

★ The faster the object moves the more streamlined it needs to be

Questions

1 How are modern cars and vehicles made more streamlined?

2 Make a drawing of a racing car.

3 Why are large car ferries not streamlined?

4 Why could jumbo jets not fly at 1000 mph?

Wordbank

Streamlined – a shape which reduces friction

37 Parachutes

An interesting application of air friction is a **parachute**. A parachute has a large surface and traps a lot of air. This makes it very difficult to move quickly. Parachutes are designed to slow things down.

Historically, the Chinese were the first people to suggest the idea of a parachute jump. They built large umbrellas and jumped from special towers.

In the 15th century Leonardo Da Vinci studied birds and flight for many years. This gave him an idea for a parachute. His intention was to make a safety device so people could jump from burning buildings and survive. His drawings of the parachute show a person hanging by four wires from a large triangular canopy (Figure 1).

Figure 1 Leonardo Da Vinci's parachute

In general, parachutes are made of silk which is folded and strapped into a bag.

When people or vehicles need to slow down, a lever is pulled and the parachute is released.

It quickly fills with air and slows the object or person down dramatically.

Parachuting People

The use of parachutes to jump from great heights first began in the late 1700s, in France.

France had become seriously involved in ballooning and as a result people used to jump from balloons as part of an exhibition.

How does a parachute work?

If you jump from a great height you fall to the ground. You get faster and faster but eventually you reach a speed of about 120 mph.

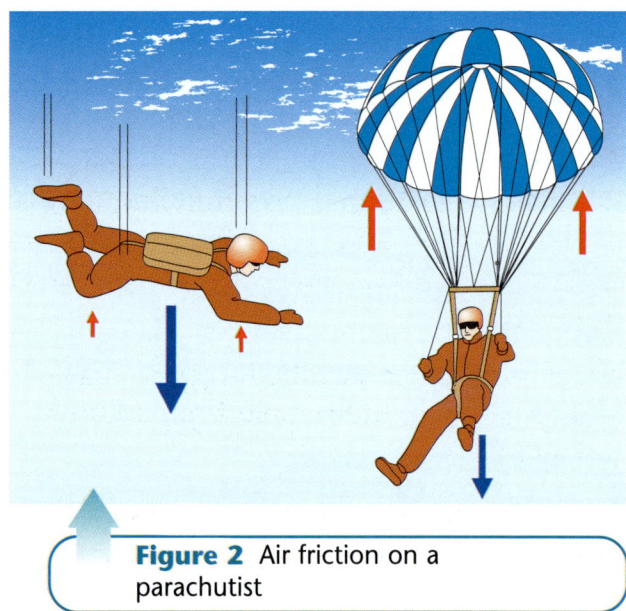

Figure 2 Air friction on a parachutist

You do not travel any faster than this speed because the air friction against your body stops you from increasing your speed.

If you then release the parachute, it opens producing a large object which causes a lot more air friction.

This slows you down even more and you then fall at about 25 mph.

This is slow enough for people to hit the ground and be able to survive.

Figure 3

Figure 4 Parachutes are used to drop emergency parcels

Other uses of parachutes

Parachutes are also used to slow down objects that have to be dropped from aircraft.

If a major disaster has occurred and people are cut off from sources of food and shelter, emergency parcels can be dropped from aircraft.

These parcels are attached to parachutes and dropped to the people from a fairly low height.

Food, clothing and blankets can be sent safely using this method.

Some fast jets need to use a parachute to help them stop. The fast jets are very streamlined and when they land they are still moving quickly. Using normal brakes (like those in a car) is not suitable. If the tyres were to stop or slow down, the aircraft would still keep moving and belly flop on the runway.

These jets release a parachute attached to the rear of the aircraft. This slows the jet down quickly.

Figure 5 A parachute slows this jet down quickly

Key ideas

★ Parachutes are used to slow things down
★ Parachutes work because they increase air friction

Wordbank

Parachute – device which increases air friction to slow things down

Questions

1 When were parachutes first used to allow people to jump from great heights?

2 How do parachutes slow something down?

3 Why do some aircraft use parachutes to slow them down?

4 List four uses of parachutes.

Weight and gravity

What is gravity?

Everyone knows that if we drop something it will fall to the ground. If you ask why it does that most people will say '**gravity**'.

Gravity pulls things to the Earth.

Why does it do that?
How does it do that?

These are very difficult questions to answer exactly. Everyone lives with gravity and its effects but we take it for granted and often do not think about it too much.

Figure 1 Imagine what it would be like without gravity?

Sir Isaac Newton is credited with 'discovering' gravity.

Figure 2 Sir Isaac Newton, born in 1642, described gravity

He was supposed to have been hit on the head by an apple and this gave him an insight into why things fall.

What do we know?

If you drop an object it will fall to the ground. As it falls it gets faster. If you drop an object from a height of 2 metres it will hit the ground at a greater speed than an object dropped from a height of 1 metre.

We all instinctively know that. That's why you would rather fall out of the bottom of a bunk bed rather than the top!

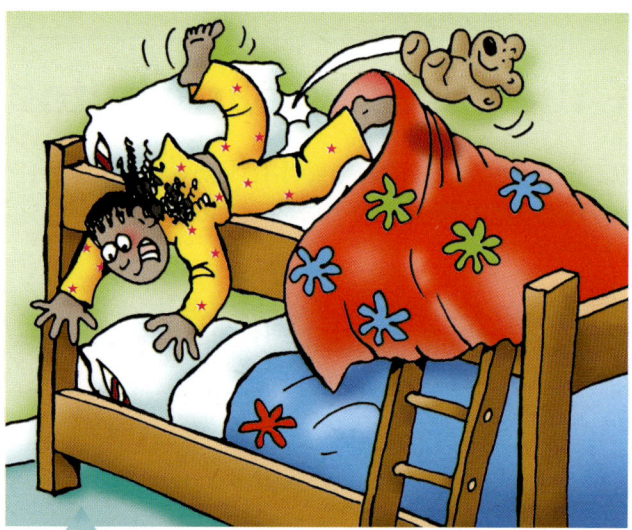

Figure 3 If you fall from the top bunk you hit the ground at a greater speed. Ouch!

What causes gravity?

Gravity is the force of attraction between two objects. All objects attract each other but with small objects the force of attraction is so weak that you cannot feel it.

Earth is a huge object and so the force of attraction between it and other objects is huge. The Earth attracts the Moon. It attracts us too! If we were on a larger planet there would be an even bigger force of attraction and this would pull us to the surface even more.

'Gravity' pulls us down to the surface of the planet. Larger objects are attracted (pulled) more than smaller objects. That is why large objects weigh more than small objects.

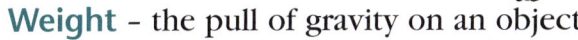
Figure 4 Large objects weigh more than small objects!

We can measure how much the Earth's gravity is pulling us by simply standing on a set of bathroom scales. The scales give a reading and tell us how much they are being squashed.

The force that the Earth's gravity pulls us to the ground is known as our **weight**.

Your weight is the 'force of gravity' on you.

How can astronauts become weightless?

At the beginning of this book we looked at what experiments scientists have been doing to prepare people for space travel. **Weightlessness** is one of the things that they have been looking at. How can people become 'weightless' if the Earth's gravity pulls them?

The simple answer is to fly far away from the Earth. The further away you are from the Earth the weaker the pull of the Earth is. If you can get far enough away the pull becomes very small and you become weightless. This is called 'zero-gravity'.

You still have all your arms, legs and so on. You haven't lost any of your body but you have no weight. (Could this be the best way to get people to lose weight?)

Key ideas

★ Gravity is a force that pulls us to the planet

★ Our weight is the force of gravity on us

★ If we leave the planet its gravity has less of an effect on us

Wordbank

Gravity – the force of attraction between two objects

Weight – the pull of gravity on an object

Weightlessness – 'zero-gravity' conditions in space

Questions

1 Write down the names of five heavy objects and five light objects.

2 What causes a planets' gravity?

3 What would happen to your weight if you were to live on a planet that was slightly smaller than Earth?

4 Why do people in Australia not fall off the Earth?

We use large amounts of energy to generate electricity which we use in homes, schools and industry.

Renewable energy sources are always being replaced.

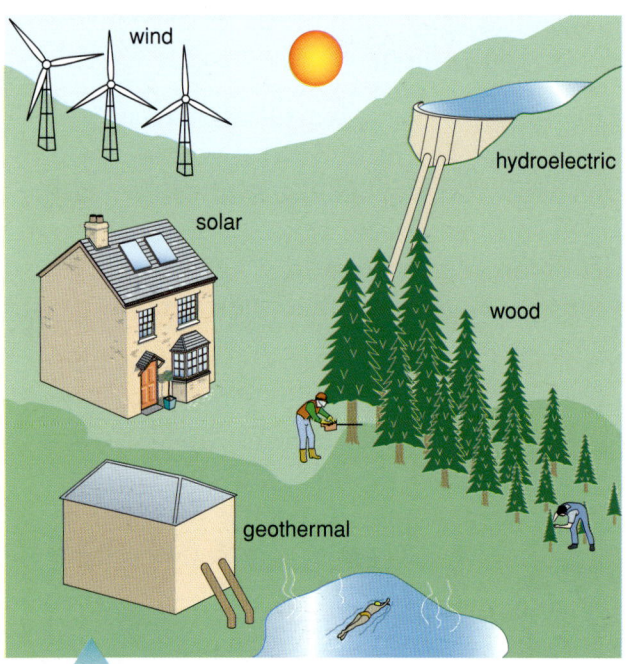

Figure 1 Renewable energy sources

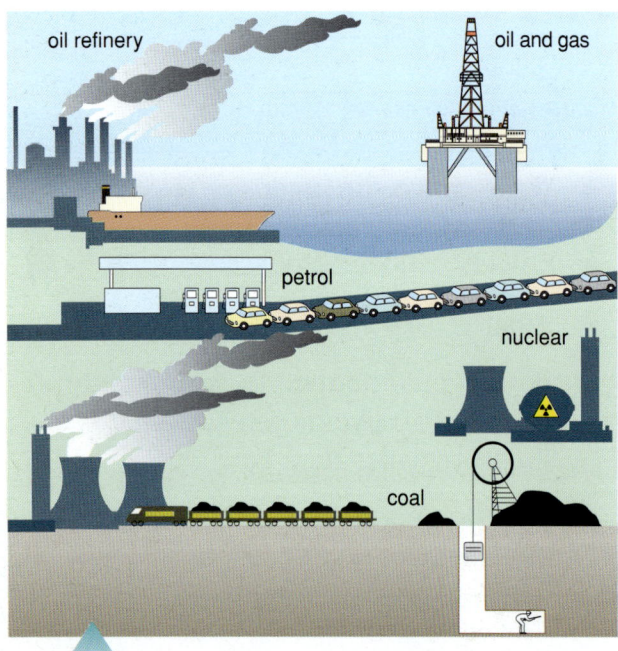

Figure 2 Non-renewable energy sources

Non-renewable energy sources cannot be replaced. They have taken millions of years to develop.

Only a small proportion of the world's energy comes from renewable sources.

Renewable	Non-renewable
10%	90%
Hydro-electricity	Coal
Solar	Oil
Geothermal	Natural gas
Wind	Nuclear

Table 1

Saving natural resources

Non-renewable energy sources are being used up faster than they can be replaced. It is important to **conserve** these natural resources or to use renewable sources to allow them to be available for future generations.

Reducing pollution

Energy conservation is also important because using non-renewable sources affect the environment. The waste from burning fossil fuels contributes to air and water pollution. Carbon dioxide released by burning contributes to the global warming of the earth. Sulphur dioxide is also made when coal is burned. It reacts with rain clouds to form 'acid rain.' which pollutes the environment.

How can you help to solve these problems?

You can change what you use:

- Walk, ride a bicycle, or use the bus or train.
- Install low energy light bulbs – they also last longer.
- Buy energy-efficient appliances.

You can change what you do.

- Turn the central heating down and use a thermostat that controls the temperature. Turn it down when you go to bed or are out of the house.

- Modern homes have well insulated walls, windows and roofs. This reduces heat loss.

- Recycle newspapers, aluminium, and plastic. Recycling uses less energy than using raw materials.

- Turn off lights, televisions and hi-fi's when leaving a room.

- Have the central heating serviced so that it works efficiently.

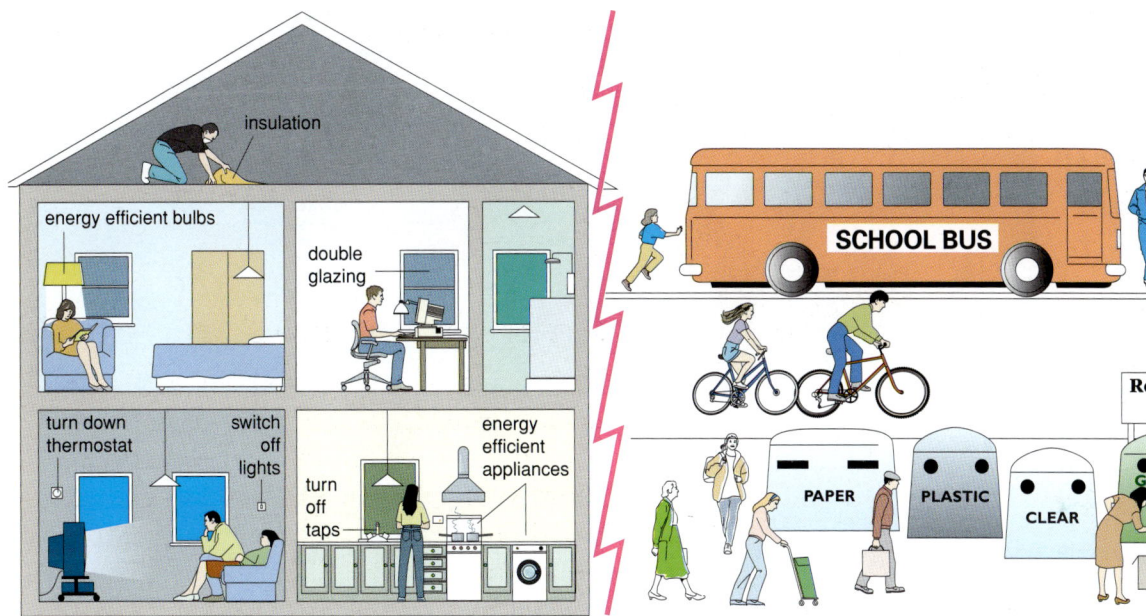

Key ideas

- ★ Two types of energy source are available to use – renewable and non-renewable sources
- ★ Natural resources are being used up too quickly and cannot be replaced
- ★ We can stop wasting energy and help save resources

Wordbank

Renewable – can be grown, or come from the weather

Non-renewable – taken from the Earth's crust and have taken millions of years to develop

Conserve – save from being wasted

Questions

1 List three non-renewable energy sources.

2 List three renewable energy sources.

3 What are the advantages of using renewable energy sources. (You can also research their disadvantages).

4 What are the advantages of using non-renewable energy sources. (You can also research their disadvantages).

5 Write an action plan.

"Things **I** can do to save energy and things **my parents** and **the government** can do to save energy".

Kenny and Karen were investigating parachutes. They made one from a plastic bag and tested it to make sure it worked.

Planning an investigation

What do you think – will the toy fall more slowly with a smaller or a bigger parachute?

Plan an investigation to find out which prediction is correct. Use these headings to help you.

1 What I want to find out?

2 The equipment I will need.

3 The way I will set it up.

4 What I will measure to find out who is correct?

Fair testing

In order to get a good result, an investigation has to be a fair test. This is how Karen and Kenny carried out their investigation:

Karen dropped the parachutes while Kenny watched to see which one hit the ground first. Is this a fair test? Why do you think so?

Collecting Evidence

In an investigation, it is important to get accurate results of the tests you do.

Karen and Kenny did not measure anything – they just observed. They decided to do the investigation again, using a stop-clock.

Why is this more scientific?

In another experiment Karen and Kenny made three parachutes of different sizes.

They tested each one three times, making sure they were all dropped from the same height.

This time they timed how long each parachute took before it reached the ground.

They put their findings in a table.

| Parachute | Time taken | | | Average |
	1st	2nd	3rd	time
A	17 sec	18 sec	16 sec	
B	12 sec	11 sec	10sec	
C	8 sec	9 sec	7 sec	

Table 1 Karen and Kenny's results

Variety is the Spice of Life

Figure 1 The surface of Earth is brimming with life

How many different kinds of living things (**species**) live on Earth? Nobody knows! One guess is that there are about a third of a million plants and half a million animals.

We can usually tell the differences between species by looking carefully at each one. The differences may be obvious e.g. size, shape or colour, but others need careful examination using a microscope.

New animals and plants are being discovered all the time.

The Vu Quang Ox

The Vu Quang (*pronounced: Voo-kwang*) Ox was recently discovered in Vietnam. It is related to cattle and goats but is unlike any other creature. It has been placed into a new group of mammals.

Figure 2 The Vu Quang Ox

The Wollemi pine

The Wollemi pine was named after the national park where they were found, less than 200 kilometres from Sydney, Australia. These pines, which were common at the time of the dinosaurs, are related to monkey-puzzle trees.

Figure 3 The Wollemi pine

Hydra

Pupils from Bell Baxter School in Cupar, Fife took part in a 'Young Scientist of the Year' competition. When they collected water samples from local hills they found a new species of *Hydra*. *Hydra* is a tiny animal that lives in water and is related to sea anemones and jellyfish.

The next discovery could be yours!

Figure 4 Hydra

Looking at similarities and differences

Some species are easy to tell apart – a magpie is very different from a robin. Some are more difficult – the chiffchaff is so similar to the willow warbler that experts must listen to their songs to be certain which one it is!

Figure 5 a) Willow warbler
b) Chiffchaff

Beech leaves and elm leaves are similar – they are flat and green and have the same general shape. Look carefully at the differences between the edge and the pattern of veins, an elm leaf also feels rough.

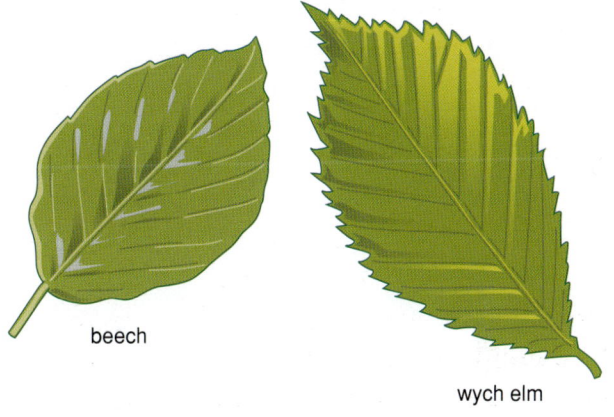

Figure 6 Beech and elm leaves are similar in shape, colour and vein pattern. The main differences are found at the base of the leaves and their edges

Key ideas

★ We do not know exactly how many other species share the planet with us

★ Visible differences such as shape, size and colour may be used to identify living things

★ Sometimes scientists need to use microscopes to identify differences between individuals which are very similar

★ New animals and plants are being discovered all the time

Wordbank

Species – groups of living things

Questions

1 Write in numbers how many plants and animals we think exist on earth.

2 Look at the following drawings and list two similarities and two differences between each pair.

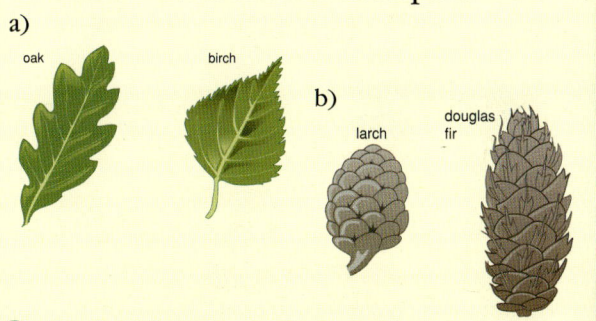

3 In the drawings above you used visible differences to identify the leaves. What other difference might scientists use?

What's its name?

When you find a plant or an animal that you do not recognise, you can look for clues that help you to identify it. For example if you are trying to identify a plant from a leaf or flower, look for clues in the colour, shape, texture or size.

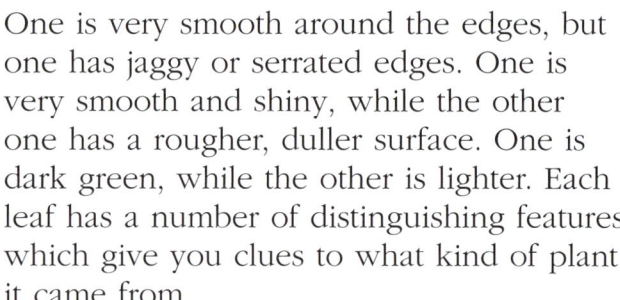

They must be in the same group because they have pink spots...er...and these must be related because they both like my lolly!?

Figure 1 Is Ross using useful features to sort these animals into groups?

What differences can you see between the two leaves in Figure 2?

One is very smooth around the edges, but one has jaggy or serrated edges. One is very smooth and shiny, while the other one has a rougher, duller surface. One is dark green, while the other is lighter. Each leaf has a number of distinguishing features which give you clues to what kind of plant it came from.

If you are trying to identify an animal, ask yourself these questions:

1   What kind of body covering does it have – hair, feathers or scales?

2   Does it have legs (if so how many) wings or fins – or no limbs at all?

3   Does it have teeth? Does it have a beak?

Answering these questions will give you clues to what kind of animal it is. Once you have found the clues, you can use a **key** to find its name. Keys are based on the similarities and differences in the appearance of living things.

Using keys

Look carefully at this small pond animal and identify its main features.

laurel

elm

Figure 2 a) Laurel leaf b) Elm leaf

Figure 3 Ramshorn snail

In this key you have to follow the clues until you come to its name.

This kind of key is called a branched key because it has lots of branches, just like a tree.

When you are using a key like this, you have to observe the main features of your mystery animal or plant very carefully. For example it is sometimes easy to think that small hairs on a small animal are legs, or to count parts of its tail as legs. This animal has only six legs, but you might think that it had eight or ten, if you did not look carefully.

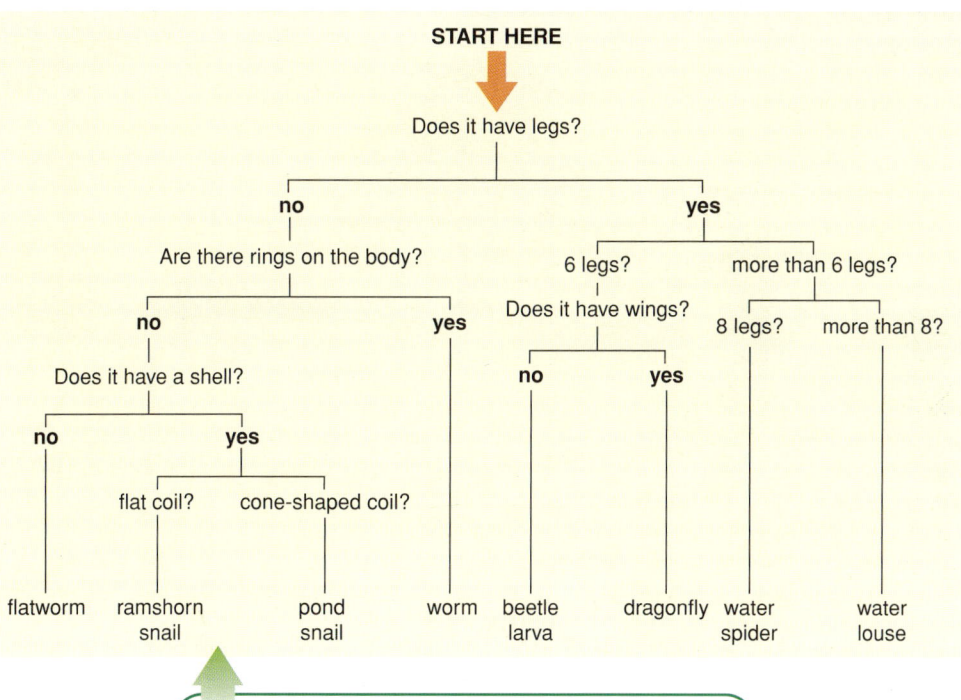

START HERE

Does it have legs?

- no
  - Are there rings on the body?
    - no
      - Does it have a shell?
        - no → **flatworm**
        - yes
          - flat coil? → **ramshorn snail**
          - cone-shaped coil? → **pond snail**
    - yes → **worm**
- yes
  - 6 legs?
    - Does it have wings?
      - no → **beetle larva**
      - yes → **dragonfly**
  - more than 6 legs?
    - 8 legs? → **water spider**
    - more than 8? → **water louse**

Figure 4 A branched key

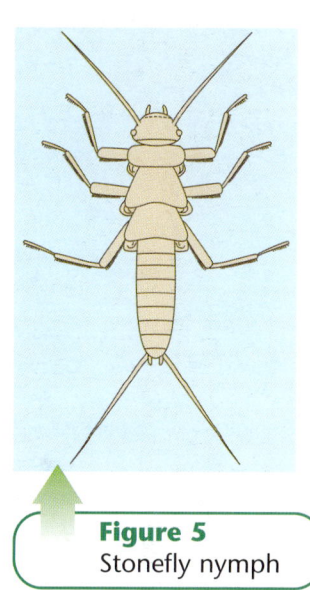

Figure 5
Stonefly nymph

Key ideas

- ★ The appearance of a plant or animal provides clues to its identity
- ★ Keys help you identify an unknown plant or animal
- ★ Keys focus on the similarities and differences in the appearance of living things
- ★ To use a key successfully, you have to observe your unknown animal or plant very carefully

Wordbank

Key – a tool used to identify unknown plants and animals

Questions

1 Identify three differences between these two animals.

2 What is a key used for?

3 Why is this key called a branched key?

4 Use the branched key to identify these two pond animals:

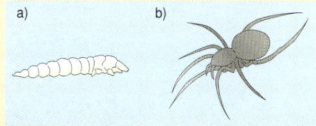

5 What clues did you use to identify them?

Plants can be grouped according to whether they produce **flowers** or not. Flowers are important in **reproduction**, the process by which new individuals are made. Flowers are often brightly coloured and scented to attract insects.

Here are some flowering plants that you are probably familiar with:

Figure 1 Flowering plants

There are many plants that produce flowers which are not brightly coloured. Because their flowers are not obvious you may not think they are flowering plants, but they are. Here are some of them.

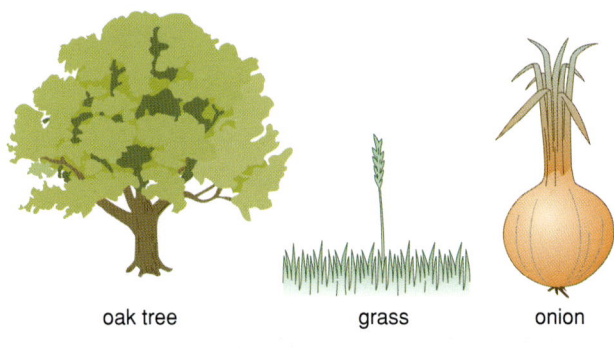

Figure 2 Not so obvious flowering plants

All flowering plants have five main parts:

- **stems**
- **leaves**
- **roots**
- **flowers**
- **seeds**.

Each of these has a particular job.

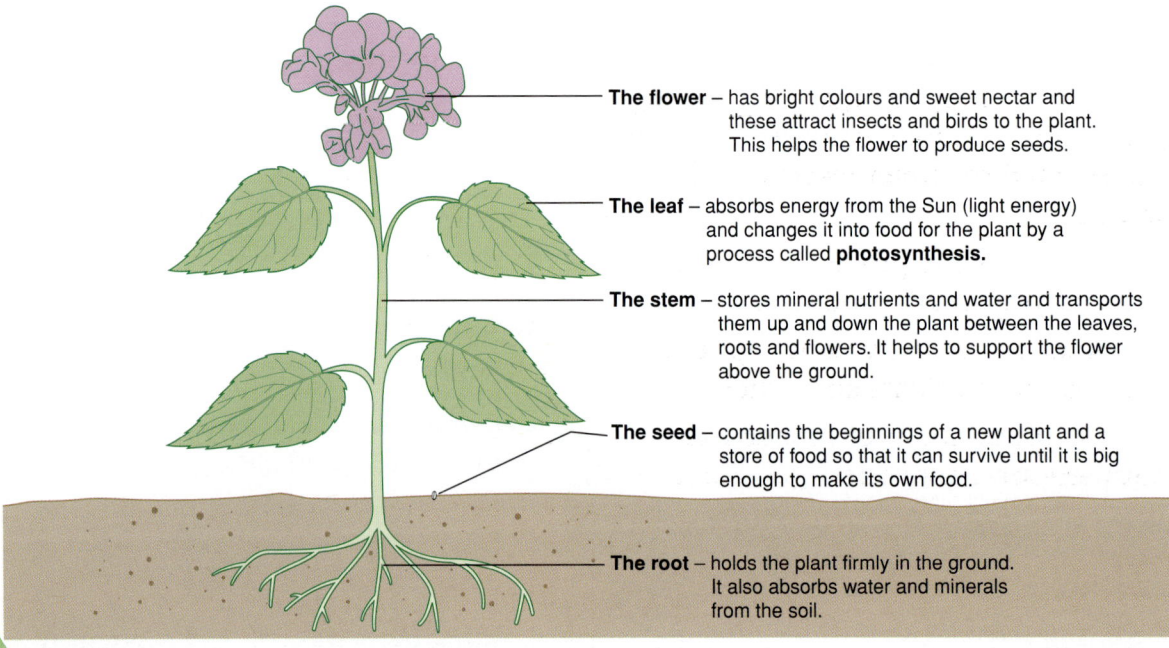

The flower – has bright colours and sweet nectar and these attract insects and birds to the plant. This helps the flower to produce seeds.

The leaf – absorbs energy from the Sun (light energy) and changes it into food for the plant by a process called **photosynthesis.**

The stem – stores mineral nutrients and water and transports them up and down the plant between the leaves, roots and flowers. It helps to support the flower above the ground.

The seed – contains the beginnings of a new plant and a store of food so that it can survive until it is big enough to make its own food.

The root – holds the plant firmly in the ground. It also absorbs water and minerals from the soil.

Figure 3 Each part of a flowering plant has a job

Flowering plants can be very big or very small and so can their flowers and seeds. Some flowers are so small you need a magnifying glass to see them.

The smallest flower is produced by a species of duckweed. The plant itself measures only 0.5–1.2 mm long!

While this flower is almost one metre in diameter!

Figure 4 Rafflesia produces the largest flower on Earth. It grows in the tropical rainforest

Key ideas

★ Flowering plants include large trees and tiny grasses as well as the more familiar plants that we see in gardens and woods

★ Flowering plants have five main parts – flowers, seeds, leaves, stems and roots

★ Each part has a particular role in keeping the plant healthy

★ Flowers are important in plant reproduction

Wordbank

Flower – reproductive organ of plants; often brightly coloured and scented to attract insects and birds

Reproduction – the process by which new individuals are produced

Root – anchors the plant to the ground and absorbs nutrients and water

Stem – supports the plant; water and nutrients are transported through it to the leaves

Leaf – makes the food the plant needs

Seed – the beginnings of a new plant

Photosynthesis – the process by which plants make their own food

Questions

1 What do the roots provide to help the plant grow?

2 Why is the stem so important to a plant?

3 Copy this diagram of a flowering plant and label the five main parts.

Non-flowering plants

There are a number of groups of plants that do not reproduce using flowers. Some of the ones you will recognise are mosses, ferns and conifers.

Mosses

Figure 1 Moss with tall capsules

Moss plants have small, thin stalks and leaves. They do not have roots like flowering plants but cling onto the surface of trees and rocks using tiny hair-like **filaments**. New moss plants grow from tiny **spores**. These are produced by the moss plant and are kept safe in small **capsules**.

Because they do not have roots, moss plants may dry out if rainfall is low. As a result, mosses live in wet places.

Ferns

Figure 2 Ferns grow in damp, shady places

Ferns are amongst the oldest groups of plants that grow on Earth. Fossils of ferns which lived may millions of years ago have been found in rocks. Most ferns like to grow in damp, shady places. Unlike flowering plants, many ferns do not have stems but grow directly from the ground, with long feathery leaves, or **fronds**.

On the underside of these fronds you can see small brown spots. Inside the brown spots there are many tiny spores. These spores contain the beginnings of a new fern. When the leaves dry out, the spores are released and travel through the air. If they land in moist soil the spores will grow into new plants away from the parent.

Figure 3 When the leaves dry out, the spores are catapulted through the air

Conifers

Figure 4 This Scots Pine tree is a conifer

Trees such as pine, larch, spruce and yew are conifers. Instead of flowers, they produce **cones** and these contain the seeds. Each seed contains the beginning of a new plant inside, with a supply of food to start it growing.

The leaves of conifers are usually needle-shaped or shaped like scales. Nearly all conifers are evergreen – this means that they keep their leaves all the year round.

Figure 5 These cones are on a tree

Figure 6 A mature cone contains seeds

Key ideas

★ Non-flowering plants include mosses, ferns and conifers

★ New ferns and mosses grow from tiny spores rather than seeds

★ Conifers produce cones and these contain the seeds for the new trees

Wordbank

Filaments – thin thread-like parts of mosses

Spores – the tiny beginnings of new mosses and ferns

Fronds – the long feathery leaves of ferns

Cones – the part of the conifer that contains the seeds of the new tree

Questions

1 Where are you most likely to find mosses? Why?

2 Name two differences between mosses and flowering plants.

3 Where can you find the spores on fern plants?

4 Conifers are described as 'evergreen'. What does this mean?

5 Describe how mosses and ferns reproduce.

6 Why are spores catapulted through the air so that they land away from the parent plant?

The human body is a collection of **systems** working together.

Each system is made up of a collection of **organs**.

Each organ is, in turn, made up of different **tissues**.

Each tissue is made of **cells**. All living things are made up of cells.

cells→tissues→organs→systems→body

The Nervous System

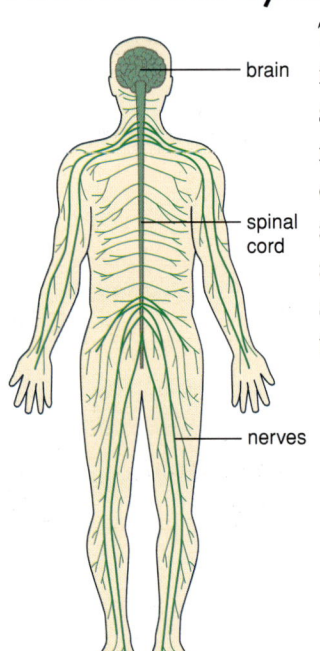

brain

spinal cord

nerves

The nervous system includes the brain, spinal cord and the nerves. This system carries information around the body. It allows the body to sense and respond to the environment.

The Respiratory System

The respiratory system includes the nose, windpipe and lungs. This system carries out breathing. Oxygen gas is absorbed into the blood from the air that we breathe into our lungs. Carbon dioxide is removed from the blood, and returned to the air when we breathe out.

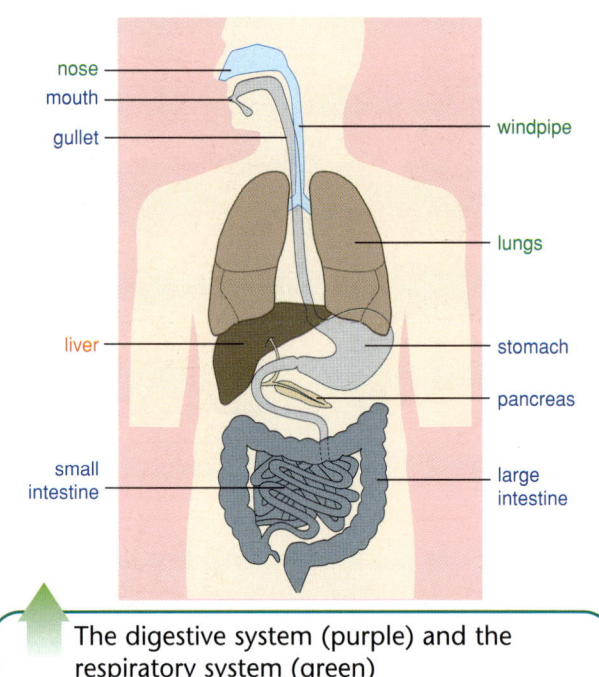

nose

mouth

gullet

windpipe

lungs

liver

stomach

pancreas

small intestine

large intestine

> The digestive system (purple) and the respiratory system (green)

The Circulatory System

The circulatory system includes blood, blood vessels and the heart. This system transports materials around the body. Oxygen and food is carried by the blood to where it is needed in the body. Waste materials, such as carbon dioxide, are taken to where they are removed from the body.

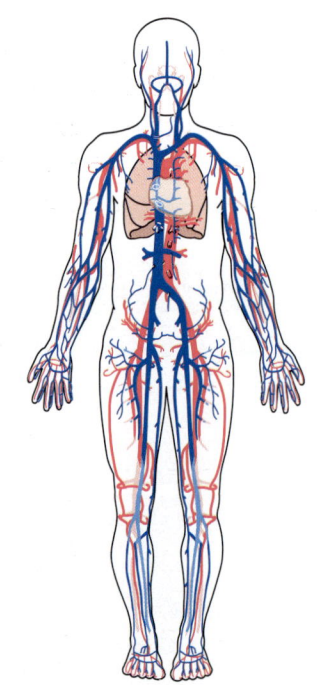

The Digestive System

The digestive system includes the mouth, gullet, stomach and intestines. This system breaks down food into simple, **soluble** materials. These are then absorbed into the blood and transported around the body.

The Reproductive System

The reproductive system includes male or female organs which produce special sex cells. These sex cells join together and develop into babies.

The Skeletal System

The skeletal system includes bones, muscles, ligaments and tendons. These work together to support and move the body. Some bones are also arranged in a way which provides protection for some organs of the body. For example the lungs and the heart are protected by the rib cage and the brain is protected by the skull.

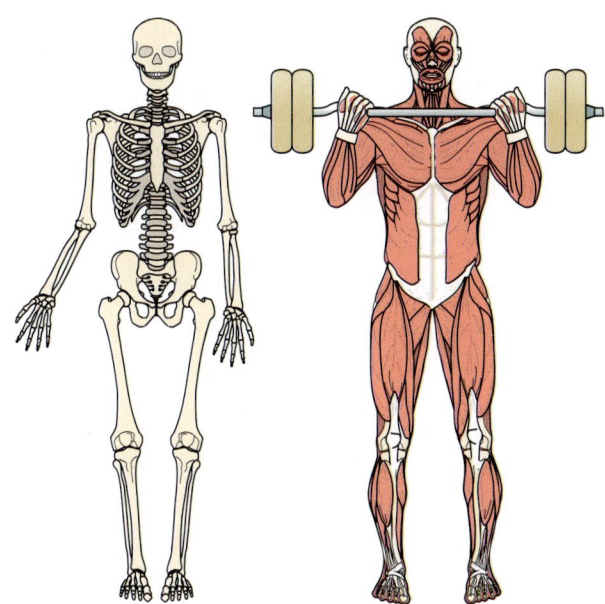

The Excretory System

The excretory system includes the kidneys and the bladder. This system removes waste from the blood. The liver is linked to this system and it turns poisonous chemicals in the blood into harmless ones. Some of these are removed by the kidneys.

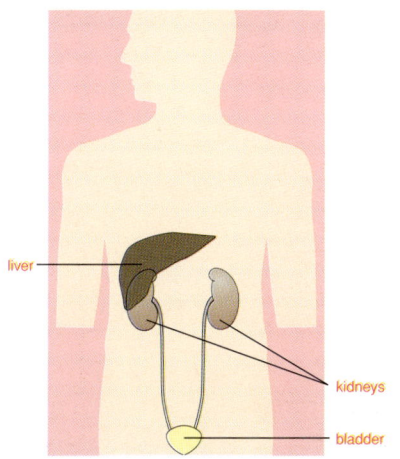

Key ideas

★ The body is made up of several systems working together

★ Systems are made from organs, organs from tissues and tissues from cells

Wordbank

Cells – basic unit of living things

Tissues – group of cells working together

Organs – group of tissues working together

Systems – group of organs working together

Soluble – material able to dissolve into a solution

Questions

1 Draw an outline of the human body and label the position of the following organs:

a) heart b) brain c) stomach
d) ear   e) rib cage f) kidneys
g) lungs

2 Arrange the following in order, starting from the smallest to the largest:

circulatory system muscle tissue
the heart muscle cells

3 Suggest two organs which are protected by the skeletal system.

4 Name three organs which allow the nervous system to sense the environment.

5 Name two substances transported by the circulatory system.

91

Breathing is the process of air passing from outside the body into the lungs and back out again.

We have to breathe to get the oxygen the body needs to stay alive.

Breathing also removes carbon dioxide, which we make as a waste product.

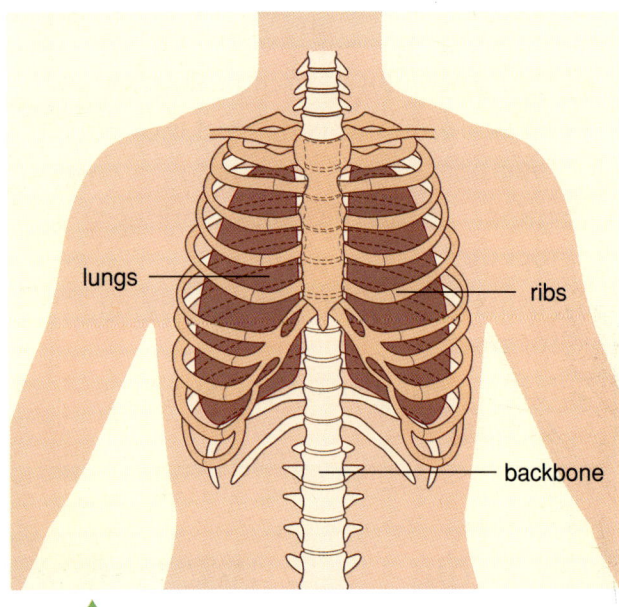

Figure 1 The lungs are inside the chest

We use the lungs for breathing.

Both lungs are found inside the chest. They are surrounded by the ribs which form a protective cage around them (Figure 1).

Each breath of air travels through a system of tubes in the order shown in Figure 2.

Some of the **oxygen** passes from the **inhaled** air into the blood at the air sacs.

At the same time **carbon dioxide**, a waste gas made by the body, passes out of the blood and into the **air sacs**. Air with extra carbon dioxide is **exhaled** from the body.

When we inhale the lungs increase in volume as they fill with air. Some people breathe in as much as three litres in each breath.

When we exhale, the volume of the lungs reduces as they empty.

Muscles between the ribs and **diaphragm** carry this out.

Figure 2 The movement of air when we breathe

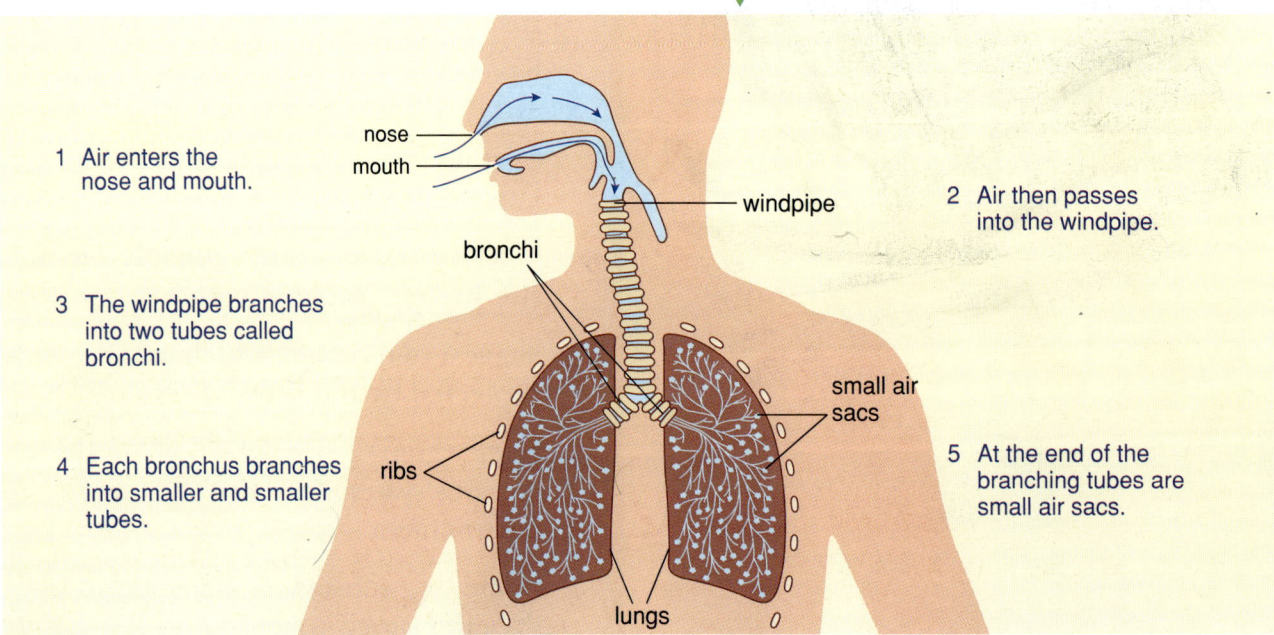

1 Air enters the nose and mouth.

2 Air then passes into the windpipe.

3 The windpipe branches into two tubes called bronchi.

4 Each bronchus branches into smaller and smaller tubes.

5 At the end of the branching tubes are small air sacs.

a)

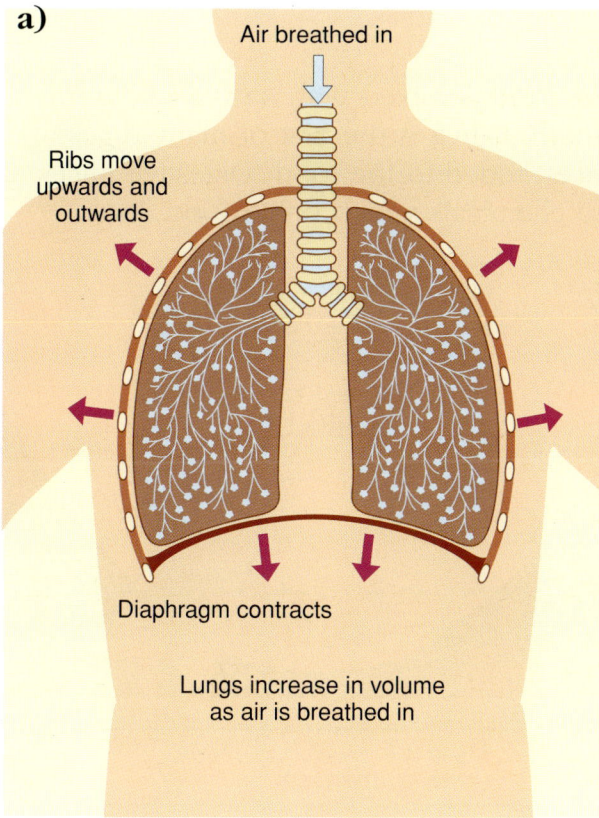

Air breathed in

Ribs move upwards and outwards

Diaphragm contracts

Lungs increase in volume as air is breathed in

b)

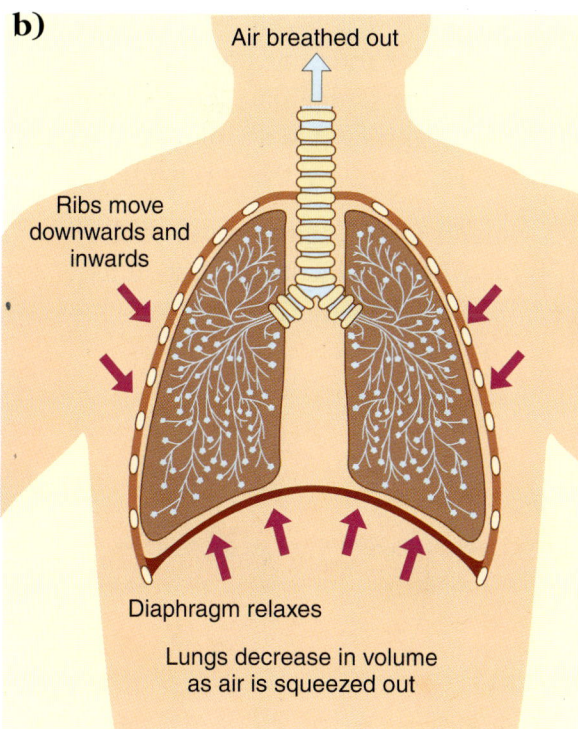

Air breathed out

Ribs move downwards and inwards

Diaphragm relaxes

Lungs decrease in volume as air is squeezed out

Figure 3 The shape of the lungs during **a)** inhalation and **b)** exhalation

Key ideas

★ The lungs are the organs for breathing. They are found in the chest

★ Air passes into the lungs through a system of tubes

★ Oxygen gas is removed from the air at the air sacs

★ Carbon dioxide gas is added to the air at the air sacs

Wordbank

Inhalation – process of breathing in

Exhalation – process of breathing out

Windpipe – tube connecting nose to lungs

Bronchi – branching tubes from windpipe into lungs

Air sacs – found at the end of the system of branching tubes in the lungs

Oxygen – gas removed from air during breathing

Carbon dioxide – gas added to air during breathing

Diaphragm – muscle involved in breathing

Questions

1 Where are the lungs located?

2 What protects the lungs?

3 Describe the change in shape of the chest during:

　　a) inhalation

　　b) exhalation.

4 Describe the direction of movement of oxygen and carbon dioxide gases in the air sacs.

Digestion is the process by which food is broken down into simple, soluble substances.

Dissolved, digested food passes into the blood to provide energy and raw materials for all parts of the body.

Figure 1 Food gives us energy

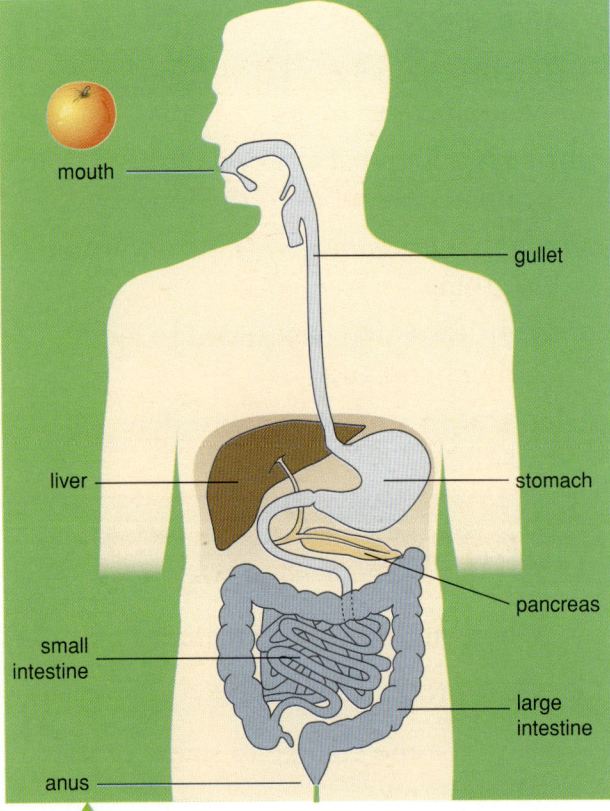

Figure 2 The digestive system

When we eat and chew food the process of digestion is started. Teeth cut and tear the food into smaller sized chunks.

The food is mixed with **saliva** in the mouth. Saliva is the first of many digestive juices added to the food. Digestive juices are chemicals which break food down.

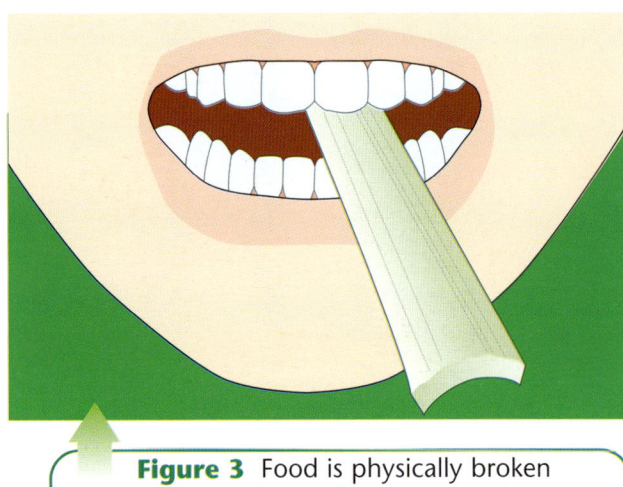

Figure 3 Food is physically broken down by the teeth

The chewed food is swallowed and passes along the **gullet** into the **stomach**. The stomach is a muscular bag which churns the food and mixes it with digestive juices which are released by the stomach.

The stomach also releases hydrochloric acid which helps digestion as well as killing bacteria in our food.

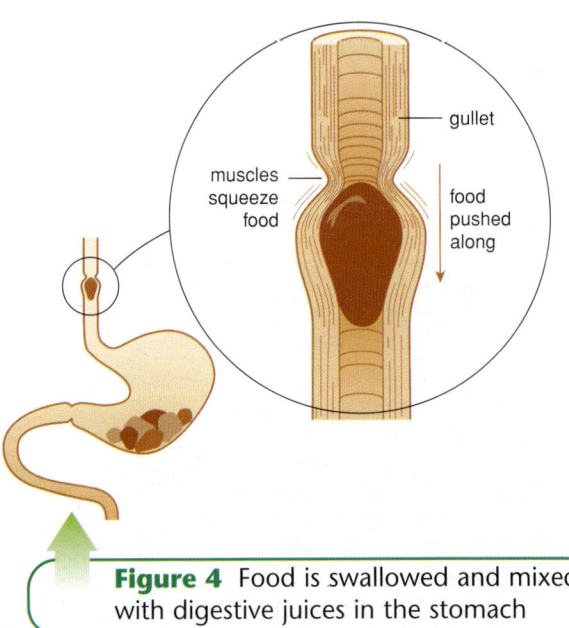

Figure 4 Food is swallowed and mixed with digestive juices in the stomach

The partly digested food passes from the stomach into the **small intestine** where digestive juices from the **pancreas** are added. By this stage the food has been turned into a smooth paste.

The food is forced along the small intestine where it continues to be digested. Fully digested food is soluble and is absorbed into the blood through the walls of the small intestine.

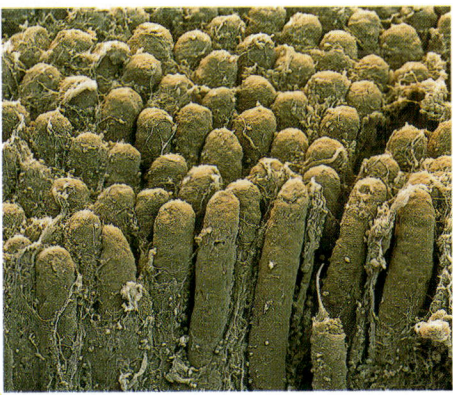

Figure 5 The wall of the small intestine has finger-like projections to absorb digested food

Undigested food travels along the **large intestine** where water is removed from it.

At the end of the large intestine the waste is stored and then expelled though the anus.

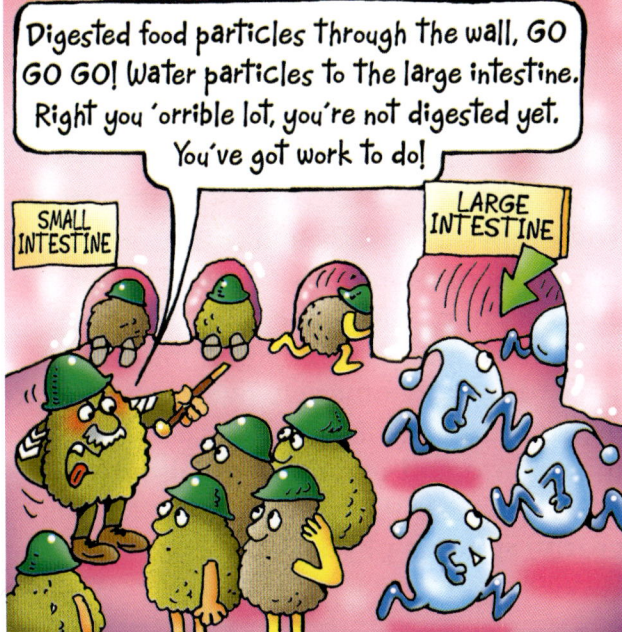

Key ideas

★ Digestion is the process of breaking food down into simpler, soluble units

★ Food is broken down physically by the teeth and chemically by digestive juices

★ Digestive juices are added at different points along the digestive system

★ The dissolved food is absorbed into the blood where it is transported around the body

Wordbank

Saliva – digestive juice produced in the mouth

Gullet – tube connecting mouth and stomach

Pancreas – organ which adds digestive juices into the small intestine

Small intestine – tube after the stomach where food is digested and absorbed

Large intestine – where water is absorbed by the body

Questions

1 Describe how the teeth help digestion.

2 Explain why food must be broken down into simple, soluble units.

3 Describe what happens to a cheeseburger as it passes through your digestive system.

4 Where is the food absorbed into the blood?

5 Why do we have hydrochloric acid in the stomach?

6 Name three organs that produce digestive juices.

Humans take a long time to reach adulthood.

During our lives our bodies go through many changes.

The rate at which we grow is different throughout our lives. A baby grows very fast. During childhood growth is fairly steady.

Between the ages of 11 and 16 boys and girls go through **puberty**. At this time growth speeds up again and the body goes through a number of changes. These changes are controlled by the release of chemicals called **hormones**. Girls normally enter puberty earlier than boys.

In girls the following body changes start in puberty:

enlargement of the breasts

the begininning of the menstrual cycle

the broadening of the hips

the appearance of hair around the sex organs and under the arms

Figure 1 Some of the physical changes that take place in girls at puberty

An important change in girls at puberty is that they begin to have **periods**. This is the beginning of the **menstrual cycle**. It is the monthly cycle during which an egg is released from the **ovary**.

In boys the following body changes start in puberty:

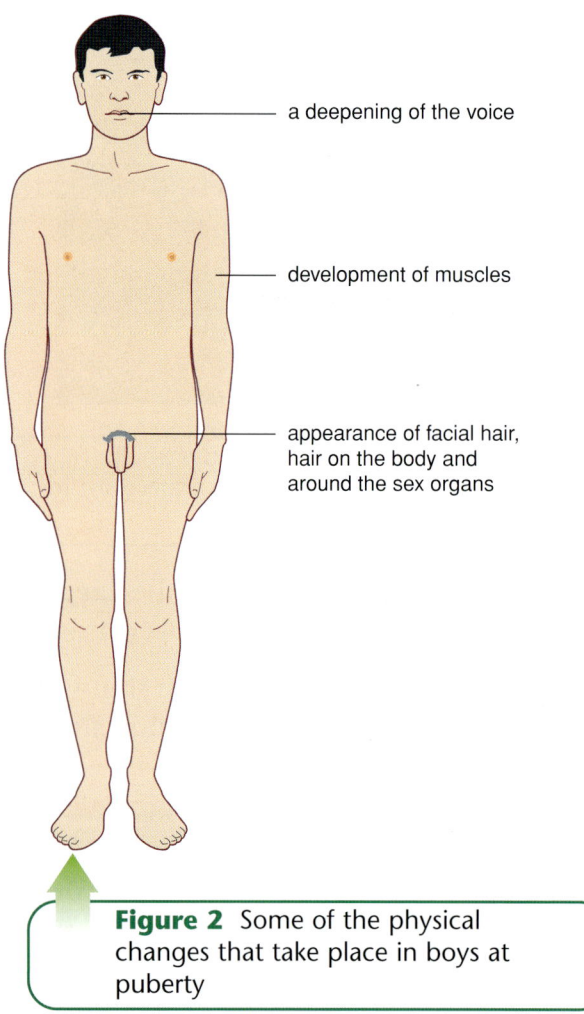

a deepening of the voice

development of muscles

appearance of facial hair, hair on the body and around the sex organs

Figure 2 Some of the physical changes that take place in boys at puberty

These physical changes mark the beginning of a stage of development called **adolescence**. This is the time when humans change from children into adults. There are many other changes occurring at the same time as these physical changes. Intelligence and emotions are also developing but they do not show the same growth spurt as physical development.

Figure 3 During puberty, boys voices 'break'. Their voices change from a high-pitch to a low-pitch

Figure 4 Sometimes the changes which occur at puberty are embarrassing

Key ideas

★ Growth happens at different speeds throughout your life

★ Puberty is a stage of development

★ Children go through puberty at different ages

★ Puberty is caused by special chemicals called hormones

Wordbank

Puberty – stage in development

Hormones – special chemicals produced by the body which control changes

Adolescence – period of change from child to adult

Menstrual cycle – monthly female cycle of periods

Ovary – female sex organ which releases eggs

Questions

1 Suggest two ages when growth in the human body is rapid.

2 Between what ages does puberty normally take place?

3 What changes would be expected in the female body at puberty?

4 What changes would be expected in the male body at puberty?

5 Name two other forms of development which do not keep pace with the physical growth spurt during puberty?

Reproduction is the process by which new individuals are made.

Figure 1 Is this how new babies are made?

Humans reproduce by **sexual reproduction**, which involves both a male and a female.

Figure 2 Sexual reproduction involves a male and a female

Sexual reproduction needs special cells. The male sex organ, the **testes**, makes the male sex cell which is called a **sperm**. The female sex organ, the **ovary**, makes the female sex cell which is called an **ovum**. During **fertilisation** they come together.

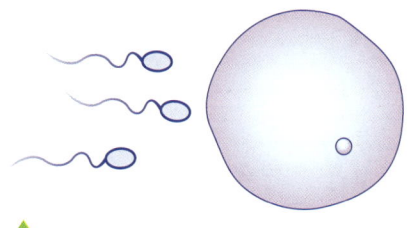

Figure 3 The male sperm are about to fertilise the female egg

When the sperm and ovum join together, the new cell starts to grow. This takes place inside the mothers' body. The fertilised ovum attaches onto the wall of the **womb**. Here it develops as an **embryo**.

After 8 weeks it is called a **foetus** and is about 2.5 cm long. By 12 weeks it is 5 cm long. At 24 weeks the foetus averages 20 cm and weighs close to 800 g. Development continues until 40 weeks when the baby is born.

a)

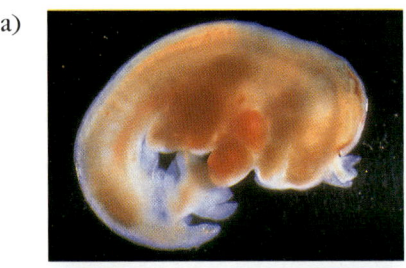

b)

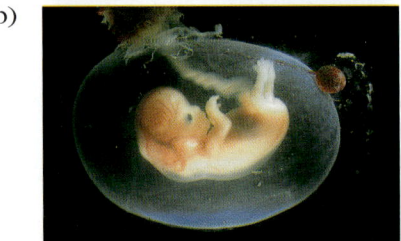

c)

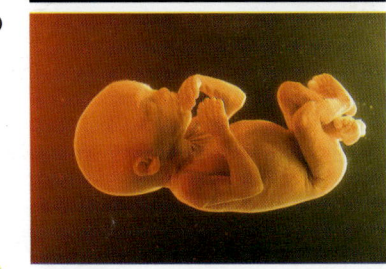

Figure 4 Development of a foetus in the womb a) 4 weeks b) 8 weeks c) 23 weeks

The developing baby gets food from the mother through the **umbilical cord** which attaches the baby to the mother's womb.

After birth the baby is looked after by the parents. This period of care takes many years until the human has passed through adolescence to become an adult.

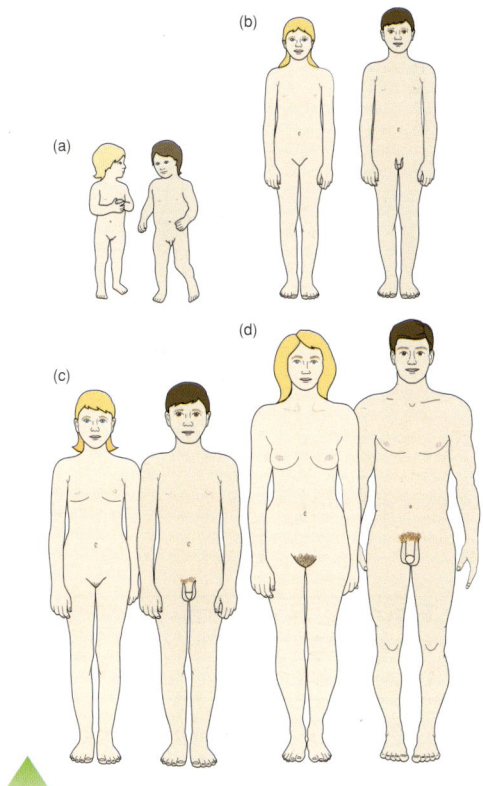

Figure 5 The development from infant to adult

Figure 6 The development from infant to adult takes many years. It involves physical, mental and emotional changes – fortunately for these parents!

Key ideas

★ Reproduction is the process by which new individuals are formed

★ The male sperm joins with the female ovum in a process called fertilisation

★ The fertilised egg grows within the womb of the female

★ Development of the foetus lasts for 40 weeks

★ Care is provided by parents for many years after the baby is born

Wordbank

Reproduction – production of new individuals

Testes – male sex organ

Ovary – female sex organ

Sperm – male sex cell

Ovum – female sex cell

Fertilisation – process when sex cells join together

Womb – site of development of baby inside the mothers' body

Embryo – early stage of development

Foetus – an embryo over 8 weeks old

Umbilical cord – organ joining embryo to mother through which it gets nutrients

Questions

1 What are the names of the male and female sex cells?

2 What term is used to describe when the sex cells join together?

3 How long does development normally take inside the womb?

4 What is the purpose of the umbilical cord?

50 The flower

Plants can be classified as flowering or non-flowering plants. Flowering takes place so that plants can reproduce. Flowers contain male and female parts which produce sex cells. The sex cells combine to form seeds which grow into new plants. Because both male and female sex cells are involved this is called sexual reproduction.

Many different flowers exist but they all have the same general structure.

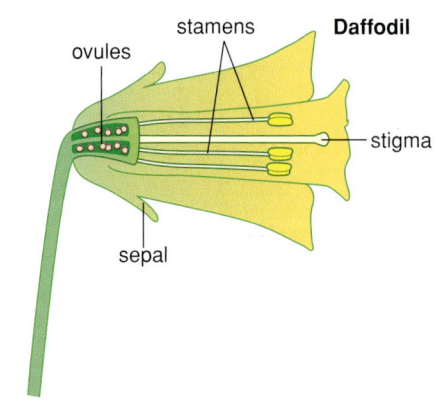

Daffodil

ovules
stamens
stigma
sepal

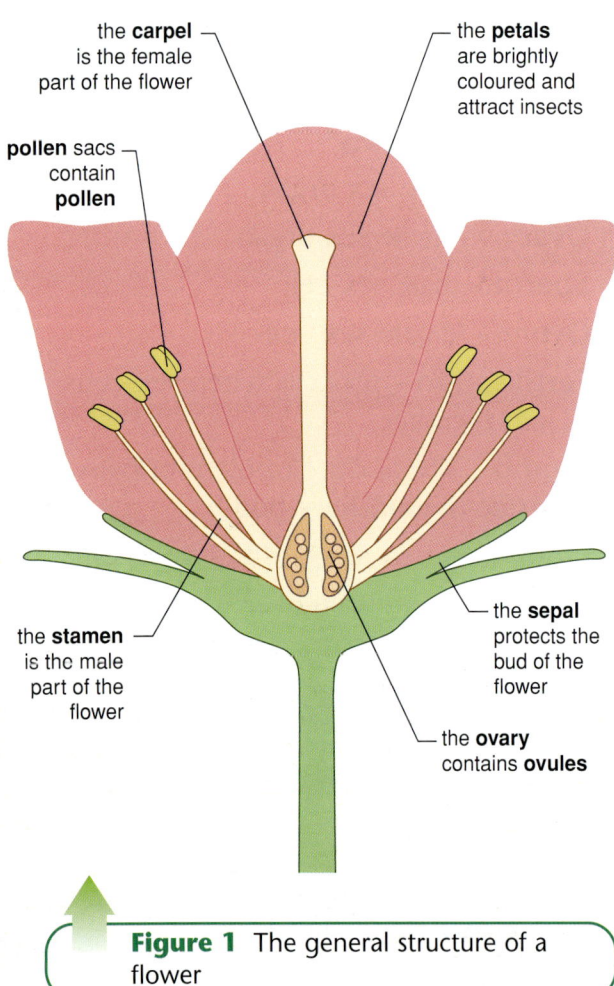

the **carpel** is the female part of the flower

the **petals** are brightly coloured and attract insects

pollen sacs contain **pollen**

the **stamen** is the male part of the flower

the **sepal** protects the bud of the flower

the **ovary** contains **ovules**

Figure 1 The general structure of a flower

ray flowers
disk flowers
ray flowers
disk flowers

Figure 2 Flowers can be different shapes but they all have the same general structure

The male sex cell in flowers is **pollen**. These are tiny cells which are found in the tip of the stamen.

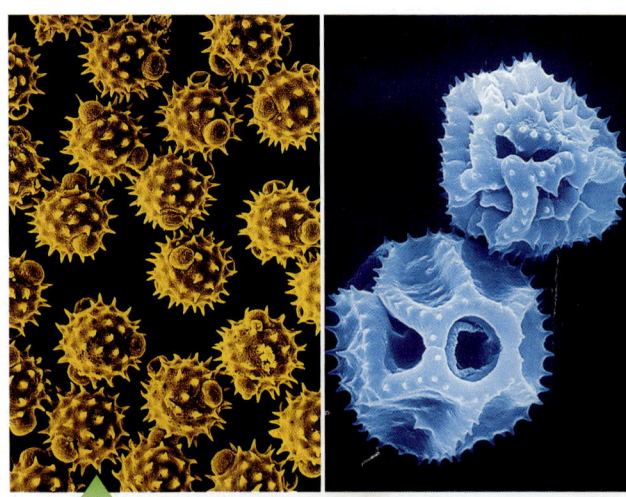

Figure 3 Different species have different shaped pollen grains. Scientists can identify plants by looking at the shape of the pollen

Daffodils, tulips and daisies and snapdragons are all different species of flowering plants but if you look carefully at them you can see similarities. They all have **petals**, **carpels**, **stamens** and **sepals**, they are just arranged differently.

The female sex cells are called **ovules** and these are found at the base of the carpel.

Plants will only release their pollen when the conditions are favourable, usually when it is warm and dry.

Fertilisation occurs when a pollen grain and an ovule meet. When this happens the new cell grows and becomes a seed. Shortly after fertilisation much of the outer part of the flower shrivels and falls off. For example apple and cherry blossom can form litter on our streets.

The remaining parts continue to grow into fruits and seeds.

The seeds can then be scattered and grow into new plants in the following year.

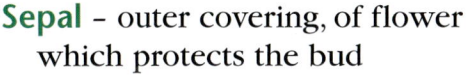

Figure 4 Ovules in the ovary of a flower

Key ideas

★ Flowers can be different shapes and sizes but they all have the same general structure

★ Flowers carry out sexual reproduction

★ In flowering plants male sex cells are called pollen and female sex cells are called ovules

★ Fertilisation is when the pollen and ovule combine to form a seed

Wordbank

Petal – colourful part of flower which attracts insects

Sepal – outer covering, of flower which protects the bud

Stamen – male part of flower where pollen grains are made

Carpel – female part of flower where ovules are made

Pollen – the male sex cell

Ovule – the female sex cell

Questions

1 Make a drawing of a flower and mark on it: petal, sepal, stamen and carpel.

2 Use any of the following terms to complete the following sentences:

**petals   pollen   protect   carpels
insects   ovules   sepals
sex cells   stamen**

a) The male part of the flower is called the _____. This is the part where _____ is made.

b) The female part of the flower is called the _____. This is the part where _____ are made.

c) Pollen and ovules are _____.

d) Buds are surrounded by _____ which _____ the flower as they grow.

e) Colourful _____ attract _____ and fall off when the seeds start to grown.

Pollination is the process of how pollen travels from the stamen of one flower to the ovules inside the carpel of a different flower.

The stamen

When we look at the stamen more closely we can see that it has two main parts – the **anther** and the **filament**.

Figure 1 The pollen is made in pollen sacs inside the anther. Pollen is released when the anther ripens and splits open

Pollen grains are incredibly small. Each anther produces millions of grains. Since they are small they can be spread easily.

Pollination by insects

Many flowers have brightly coloured petals which attract insects. The insects are also attracted by the scent of **nectar**.

Figure 2 Pollen sticks to the legs of the bee and is carried to another flower

Bees and other insects visit flowers in order to collect the sugary nectar which is found at the base of the petals. Once inside the flower the pollen sticks to their bodies. When the bee visits other flowers some of the pollen is transferred to the carpel.

Figure 3 This flower attracts bees by looking like a female bee!

How does pollen reach the ovules?

When the female part of the flower is ready to be fertilised the tip of the carpel becomes 'sticky'. If a pollen grains land there it will stick. The pollen grain then grows a long tube which pushes down inside the carpel towards the ovule. Fertilisation takes place when the pollen tube reaches the ovule. The fertilised ovule grows into a seed which contains a store of food for the new plant.

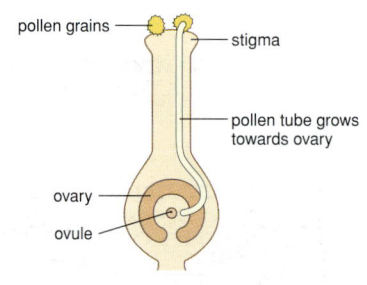

Figure 4 Pollen tube grows down through the carpel to reach the ovule

Pollination by wind

Pollen can be transported by the wind. Ripe anthers split and the pollen grains are released into the air. The wind can carry the pollen great distances to other flowers of the same kind.

Figure 5 Pollen can be transported long distances by the wind

These plants do not have colourful flowers because they do not need to attract insects.

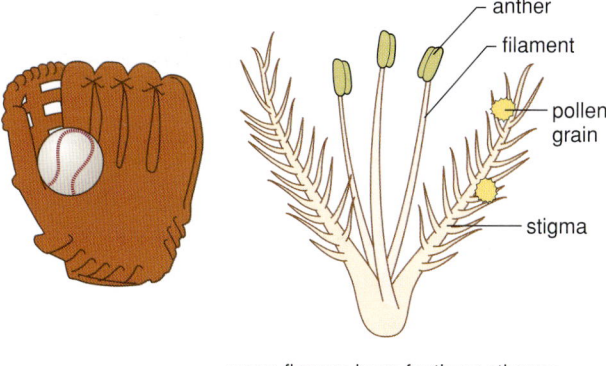

anther

filament

pollen grain

stigma

grass flowers have feathery stigmas to catch the wind-blown pollen

Figure 6 Carpels of wind pollinated flowers, such as grasses, are designed to catch pollen

The carpel is designed to catch the pollen – rather in the same way as a baseball glove is designed to catch a ball.

Key ideas

★ Pollen is made and stored in sacs in the anther

★ Ripe anthers split and pollen is released

★ Pollen is carried by insects or by the wind

★ A pollen grain landing on a carpel grows a pollen tube and fertilises the ovule

Wordbank

Pollination – how pollen is transferred from one flower to another

Anther – top end of stamen where pollen is made and stored

Filament – stem of the stamen

Nectar – sugary material that attracts insects

Questions

1 Draw and label a stamen showing where the pollen is made.

2 Describe two ways that pollen can move from one flower to another.

3 What happens to the pollen that reaches the stigma?

4 Explain why some flowers are brightly coloured and others are not.

5 Compare the appearance of the carpels and stamens of wind and insect pollinated flowers.

52

Fruit formation and seed dispersal

When pollen lands on a stigma, each grain sends out a long pollen tube. This pollen tube grows through the carpel, reaches the ovary and fertilises the ovule. The ovule forms a seed. While the seed is forming, the ovary wall develops into a **fruit**.

The seed becomes surrounded by a fruit. If you open fruits you can expect to find seeds inside.

Not all fruits are edible, some are poisonous.

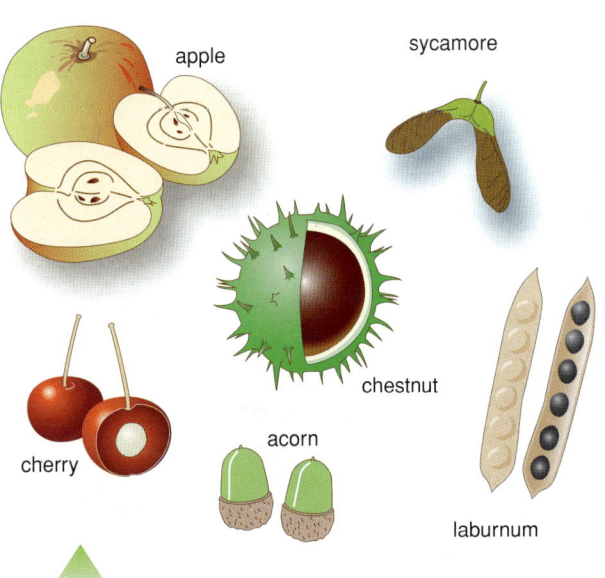

Figure 1 Which of these fruits are edible and which are poisonous?

apple
sycamore
chestnut
cherry
acorn
laburnum

The job of the fruit is to help the seeds to be spread over a wide area. This is called **dispersal**. If the seeds are not dispersed, all the new plants will grow in the same area and become overcrowded. Dispersal gives each plant a better chance of survival.

Seed Dispersal

Seeds can be dispersed in a number of ways – the fruit plays the major role in this. They can help with animal or wind dispersal.

1   Eaten by animals

Some fruits are brightly coloured and are good to eat. As the fruit grows it also ripens. Ripe fruits attract animals. (YUM YUM!)

Figure 2 Animals disperse seeds in their droppings

When animals eat fruit they digest the soft part of the fruit but not the hard seeds. The seeds pass through the digestive system and are released by the animal in its droppings. This is usually some distance away from where the fruit was eaten.

2   Carried by animals

Some fruits are coated with little hooks. These stick to the coats of animals. They sometimes stick to the clothes of people who are walking by. When the hooks are broken the seeds fall off. This disperses the seeds.

Figure 3 Having fun with 'sticky Willie's' helps to spread their seeds

3 Carried by wind

Some seeds are dispersed by the wind. These seeds are light and are often shaped to fly in the wind. This allows them to be blown for large distances away from the original plant.

Figure 4 Seeds dispersed by wind

Key ideas

★ Fruits are formed around seeds
★ Fruits enable seed dispersal
★ Seeds can be dispersed by animals or wind

Wordbank

Dispersal – to be spread over a wide area

Fruit – part of the plant which has grown from the flower to disperse the seed

Questions

1 Describe how seeds may be dispersed by animals that have eaten some fruit.

2 How do animals know when the fruit is ready to be eaten?

3 Describe two other ways in which seeds may be dispersed.

4 Match the seeds to the method of dispersal.

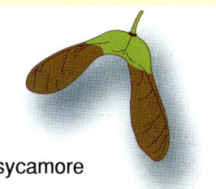
sycamore

Animal coats

burdock

Eaten by animals

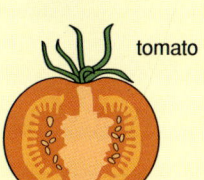
tomato

Wind

53

Human impact on the environment – Agriculture

Humans change their environment.

Britain used to be completely covered by dense forests. Britain's landscape has been changed by generations of farmers, foresters and industrialists.

The changes that humans make to their environment are generally for the benefit of the human population. Quite often, these changes harm the environment – they are described as having a **negative impact** on the environment.

One of the largest impacts that humans have on the natural environment is through agriculture – growing crops and grazing animals to produce food.

More land please!

Large areas of land are ploughed and planted with crops or grazed by animals. Using land for agriculture is called **cultivation**.

Figure 1 How has this environment been changed by humans?

Often cultivation involves cutting down the trees which would grow there naturally. This is called **deforestation**. In Brazil the rainforest is being cut down to provide land for grazing cattle.

Figure 2 Deforestation

Not all changes made by humans are bad for the environment. Some human activities can have a **positive impact** on the environment. In some areas trees are being planted (**reforestation**) to provide wood for fuel and raw materials.

Foreign crops

Most of the crops that we grow for food are not native to Britain, they were introduced from other parts of the World. For example potato plants originally came from Peru and wheat was introduced from the Middle East.

Figure 3 Most crops plants are not native to Britain

Removing **native** plants and animals to introduce crops can lead to the native species becoming endangered or even extinct.

When crops are planted they tend to be in huge fields all containing the same type of plant. This **monoculture** reduces the range of other animals and plants present.

Figure 4 Traditional meadows are becoming rare as more land is used for agriculture. The native species of wild flowers are endangered

Fertiliser and pesticides

Chemical **fertilisers** and **pesticides** are used to increase the amount of food we produce. Fertilisers contain the nutrients which plants need to grow. Pesticides prevent insects and diseases destroying crops. If farmers stopped using artificial fertiliser and pesticides, food production would drop by about 40%.

Chemical fertilisers and pesticides enter food chains and may poison animals.

The future

Humans benefit from an increase in agriculture because poverty and starvation are reduced by growing more crops. However the population of the Earth increases every year. The amount of food we produce will also have to increase. This will put even more pressure on the environment.

Key ideas

* ★ The natural environment has been changed by humans
* ★ Humans can have positive and negative effects on the environment
* ★ Agriculture has a large impact on the environment

Questions

1 Describe three ways in which food production is increased by people.

2 Explain how fertilisers and pesticides have a negative impact on the environment.

3 Make a diagram to summarise this chapter.

Wordbank

Environmental impact – the effect man has upon the environment

Cultivation – using land for growing crops

Fertilisers – chemicals that increase the growth of crops

Pesticides – chemicals that kill pests that destroy crops

54

Human impact on the environment – Water supply

There is not enough water in some parts of the world. Some people say that water will be the most important political factor in the 21st century. Wars may even be fought over future water supplies.

Irrigation

Dams are used to store and control the supply of water. Dams can have positive and negative effects on the environment.

Figure 1 Dams have a huge impact on the environment

This dam supplies water for agriculture and drinking. It also generates electricity. These are all positive effects for humans.

Agriculture

Dams are built to supply water for agriculture. This is called **irrigation**. It allows the growth of crops in areas that otherwise would be desert.

Figure 2 Irrigation allows crops to be grown

Drinking water

Clean drinking water is essential for healthy human life. Dams provides clean water for thousands of people.

Electricity

Hydro-electric power can be generated from dams. The electricity can be used to encourage industry to an area. This would provide jobs for the local people.

Dams can also have a negative impact on the environment and the people who live near it.

Homes and cultural history can be lost when artificial lakes are built. The village Bothwellhaugh was flooded when Strathclyde park was created on the River Clyde.

Habitat is destroyed and animals and plants that grow in flooded areas are lost.

Figure 3 This forest was flooded when Kariba Dam was built in Africa

Diseases are introduced to new areas when they are irrigated. Malaria is spread to new parts of the world because the mosquito, which carries malaria, breeds in slow-moving water, such as the reservoir behind dams.

Drainage – removing water

In some parts of the world there is too much water. Drainage removes water from wet places. Draining land can have a positive effect on the environment and people.

More land

Drained bogs can become farms or forests. Food grown on drained land allows the growth of population, towns and cities.

Flood prevention

Flood prevention schemes are helped by drainage. Raised river banks prevent floods.

Negative environmental impacts also results from drainage.

Habitats are destroyed by drainage. Wild plants and animals that live in the wet soil are removed and may become extinct.

Large areas of the Flow country in Sutherland have been destroyed. These wetlands have been drained and the native plant and animals are now threatened. Commercial forests have been planted to replace the natural plants and animals.

Figure 4 Commercial forests planted in the Flow Country

Villages, towns and cities may grow when bogs are drained. This process is called **urbanisation**. As the population grows in a particular area so does the pollution. Waste in the water, litter and waste in the air each affects the environment.

Key ideas

★ Water is not evenly distributed around the world
★ Humans irrigate land where there is not enough water and drain land where there is too much
★ These have positive and negative impacts on the environment and on the local people

Wordbank

Irrigation – supplying water to land
Drainage – removing water from land
Urbanisation – the development of villages, towns and cities

Questions

1 Explain three ways that dams can help people.

2 Explain how dams can harm people.

3 Describe two advantages of drainage.

4 The Three Gorges project in south west China has built a huge dam on the Yangtse River. What are the advantages and disadvantages of this project?

55

The effects of the environment on some Scottish animals and plants

All living things are affected by changes in the environment. Some environmental changes are caused by humans. Animals and plants which cannot escape from or **adapt** to suit the changing environment will be affected.

Figure 1 Are these animals adapted to their environment?

Water Vole

What are they?

Figure 2 A water vole (*Arvicola terrestris*)

Water voles live in burrows near water. They should not be mistaken as water rats.

	Rats	Voles
Nose	pointed	round
Body	sleek	round
Tail	bare	furry
Colour	brown or black	brown or black
Breed	all year	spring

Table 1 Differences between water voles and rats

How do they live?

Water voles are found near fresh water all over mainland UK. Water voles feed on water plants and, like most rodents, they mark their territory. They swim to escape from predators.

What's the problem?

Recent surveys show that the numbers of water voles have been falling. It seems that voles are only found in 2–30% of the places that they previously occupied.

Why has this happened?

One reason is because farming practices have reduced the number of waterside **habitats** suitable for the water vole. Another reason is the North American mink. These are not **native** to the UK. They have been introduced into the UK to be farmed for their fur, which is turned into coats. Over the years a large number of mink have escaped from these farms and are living in the wild. This vicious predator kills water voles inside their burrows.

Who is doing something about it?

The government is doing something. Water voles are now protected by the law. No one can damage or destroy the places where the voles live. You should help as well.

The cornflower

What are they?

Cornflowers are a native plant that was once found all over the UK. It was common in cornfields but farmers treated it as a weed. It is now very rare indeed.

Figure 3 Cornflower (*Centaurea cyanus*)

What's the problem?

The cornflower is **endangered**. This means that it risks **extinction**. Cornflower is on the official list of plants and animals that are protected.

Why has this happened?

Supplies of corn seed are much 'cleaner' than they used to be. This means that weed seeds, such as cornflower, are removed. Weed killers are widely used in farming. Any weeds growing in the field die before they are able to flower and produce seeds. So the natural cycle of cornflower growth and reproduction is broken.

Who is doing something about it?

The government is doing something. Cornflowers are now protected by the law. No one can damage or destroy the places where they grow. You should help as well.

Key ideas

★ All living things are affected by changes in their environment

★ Habitats are affected by the introduction of new species

★ Habitats are affected by change of use or agricultural practice

★ You can protect endangered species

Wordbank

Adapt – to fit into an environment

Habitat – the place where plants and animals live

Native – plant or animal which is naturally living in an area

Endangered – a plant or animal at risk of extinction

Questions

1 Make a summary note for the water vole. List five key facts. Use the mind map template below. You could use words, drawings or numbers.

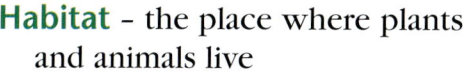

water vole

2 Make a summary note for the cornflower. List five key facts. Use the mind map template above. You could use words, drawings or numbers.

An endangered mammal – Siberian tiger

What are they?

Figure 1 Siberian tiger (Panthera tigris altaica)

Siberian tigers are the largest of the tiger subspecies.

	Sex	Mass (kilograms)	Length (metres)
Siberian tiger	male	300	3.3
	female	100–170	2.6
Sumatran tiger	male	120	2.4
	female	90	2.2

Table 1 Weight and size of two tiger species

A Siberian tiger is paler than other tigers, with brown rather than black stripes, a white chest and belly, and thick fur around its neck.

The Siberian tiger lives mainly in the woodlands of far eastern Russia and China (see Figure 2).

How do they survive?

Siberian tigers hunt elk and wild boar. Herds of elk can move as much as 40 kilometres between feeding grounds. As a result, each Siberian tigers territory is very large.

Russia

Mongolia

China

North Korea

South Korea

Key
Historical Range
Current Range

Figure 2 Range of Siberian tiger

What's the problem?

Only 360 to 400 Siberian tigers still exist in the wild but nearly 500 are managed in zoo **conservation** programmes.

Why has this happened?

Tiger body parts are used in some traditional Chinese medicine. Poachers kill them to obtain their skins and bones. Their habitat is also being turned into farmland.

Who is doing something about it?

Many agencies and organisations are promoting efforts to assist Russia in stopping the loss of the Siberian tiger. They are doing this by preserving their habitat and protecting them from poachers. A zoo breeding programme is maintaining a small and varied population. *You* should help as well.

An endangered flowering plant – Huachuca umbel

What are they?

The Huachuca umbel lives near water in the Arizona desert in Western United States. Pond edges and slowly moving parts of streams are its favoured **habitat**. It can be swept away by the rare floods that follow heavy storms. It has slender leaves that grow from underground stems. Its few flowers form a sort of umbrella shape.

How do they survive?

The main form of reproduction for this plant is from underground stems. Some seeds may form too. Their favourite habitat is where floods rarely happen.

What's the problem?

This plant is listed as an **endangered species** which means it is at risk of becoming **extinct** – and lost forever.

Why has this happened?

The introduction of cattle by ranchers has caused the margins of ponds to become trampled, damaging the plants. The removal of water for human use is causing the ponds to dry up and the habitat is lost.

Figure 3 The Huachuca umbel (*Lilaeopsis schaffneriana*)

Figure 4 Pond in Sonora desert, the habitat of the Huachuca umbel

Who is doing something about it?

The Millennium Seed Bank at the Royal Botanic Gardens, Kew in London, maintains a collection of known plant seeds. These could help with the replacement of wild populations. The United States government is trying to conserve the Huachuca umbel but some experts reckon that a single storm could be enough to remove it all together. You should help as well.

Key ideas

★ Plants and animals are endangered throughout the world
★ Extinct species cannot be replaced
★ The destruction of habitats is responsible for the extinction of living things

Questions

1 How could you change the fate of the Siberian tiger or the Huachuca umbel?

Wordbank

Endangered species – species of plants or animals which are at risk of dying out from the planet

Extinct – when no individuals of a species survive it becomes extinct

Conservation – protection of environments and species

Habitat – the environment in which a plant or animal lives

57 Responding to the environment

Living things are able to sense their environment and **respond** when it changes. Plants and animals are able to respond in many different ways to help them survive. Here are some of the changes.

Plant responses

Seasonal

Plants are able to respond to seasonal changes in temperature and daylength. (Have you noticed that the days are very short in mid-winter and very long in mid-summer?) Plants usually respond to changes in the environment by changing the way they are growing. These changes tend to occur slowly. Figure 1 shows the seasonal changes in an apple tree.

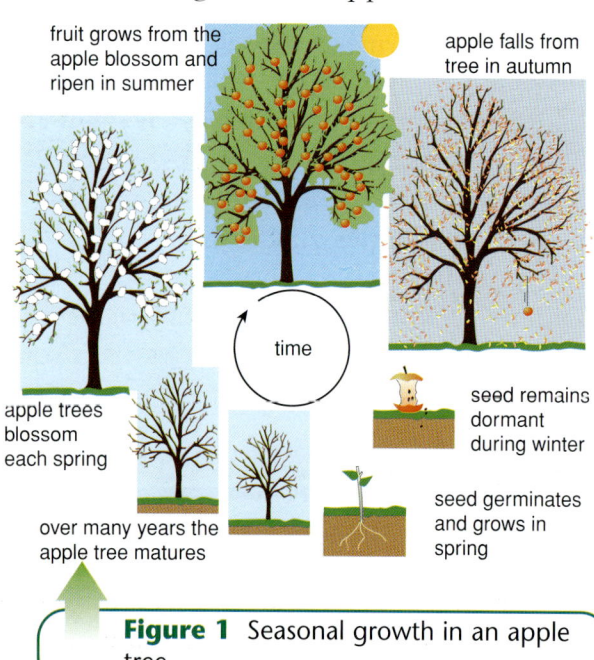

fruit grows from the apple blossom and ripen in summer

apple falls from tree in autumn

time

seed remains dormant during winter

apple trees blossom each spring

over many years the apple tree matures

seed germinates and grows in spring

Figure 1 Seasonal growth in an apple tree

Daily

For plants to grow, they need water, nutrients, light and the correct temperature. Shoots will grow towards the light and roots will grow towards water. Have you ever wondered what makes roots and shoots grow in the right direction?

Fast responses happen in some plants. This plant closes quickly and traps flies. Hairs on the surface of the leaf detect the movement of a fly. The plant responds by closing its leaves. Chemicals produced by the plant digest the insect and the plant uses the nutrients.

Figure 2 The leaves of this Venus fly trap close quickly to capture flies. Have you ever tried to catch a fly?

Animals responses

Movement is a common animal response. Animals move to avoid harmful conditions. Animal responses are generally quicker than plant responses.

Seasonal

Seasonal changes affect animals. Flocks of geese fly to Scotland each winter from the Arctic and return each spring to avoid the severe arctic winter. This is called **migration**.

Figure 3 Geese migrate to Scotland from the Arctic each winter

Other animals sleep throughout the winter – this is called **hibernation**. Birds respond to the longer days in spring and this starts courtship.

Figure 4 Swans courting in spring

Some animals turn white during the winter. In Scotland the Stoat, Ptarmigan and Mountain Hare are **camouflaged** in this way.

Daily

The daily cycle of light and darkness affect animal behaviour. **Nocturnal** owls and rodents are active at night. Sleep patterns are affected by light and dark.

Movement is the most common animal reponse.

Animals are disturbed when you lift stones in the garden. Beetles, worms and slaters quickly move away from the light.

Figure 5 Bats are nocturnal

Key ideas

★ Living things respond to the environment

★ Plants respond by growing or moving

★ Animals respond by changing their behaviour and moving away from harm

Wordbank

Respond – change in growth, movement or behaviour

Migration – seasonal movement of animals

Camouflage – disguised to blend in to surroundings

Hibernation – sleeping during the winter

Nocturnal – animal that is active during the night

Questions

1 Copy and complete the table below to match the conditions and the seasons for the apple.

Stage	Conditions	Season
flowering		
fruit formation		
seed dispersal		
seed growth		

2 What conditions might cause each of the following responses in animals:

a) hedgehogs hibernating
b) cockerels crowing
c) moths fluttering around street lights at night
d) geese flying north in spring?

Four Climbers lost in Cairngorms

Lochaber, Tuesday

Mountain rescue teams, police and RAF helicopters have not yet found the four climbers who have been missing since Sunday morning. The climbers left their cars and are believed to be poorly clothed for the conditions that have existed since the weekend. Driving snow and sub-zero temperatures...

Newspaper reports like this one are far too common. People go walking on the mountains without proper preparation and warm clothing.

If you were to go walking in the mountains, you should bring food, water, wear sturdy walking boots and warm, waterproof clothing.

Have you ever thought about how mountain animals survive the winter in the Scottish mountains?

Figure 1 A Scottish Mountain

These animals must be able to keep warm and find food even in the coldest weather. They must also avoid any animals which are trying to feed on them!

Some animals are able to survive in the mountains.

Animals which can do this are adapted to their environment.

In Scotland, the stoat, ptarmigan and mountain hare are adapted to the severe winter conditions.

Ptarmigan

Ptarmigan are small chicken-like birds. They are completely white in winter and look like the snowy ground they walk on. This **camouflages** them in the snow. Being camouflaged helps them to avoid being spotted and eaten by other animals – predators.

The feathers of the ptarmigan are waterproof and trap air. They even have feathers on their feet to help save heat.

Figure 2 A ptarmigan (*Lagopus mutus*)

Mountain hare

The mountain hare's rear feet are almost like snow shoes – with thick hair and spreading toes which allow them to move over the snow quickly and escape from predators. Air-filled winter fur gives protection against the cold.

Like the ptarmigan, the mountain hare turns white in winter to avoid predators.

Figure 3 A mountain hare (*Lepus timidus varronis*)

The Stoat

Stoats are members of the weasel family. Their coat hair is long, thick and water proof. It turns completely white in winter, apart from the black tip of the tail. The animal is called an **ermine** when the fur turns white.

Figure 4 A stoat (*Mustela erminea*)

Key ideas

★ Winter conditions in the Scottish mountains are similar to the Arctic

★ Arctic animals live in the Scottish mountains

★ Animals are adapted to their environment

Questions

1 Describe the weather conditions that can appear in the Scottish mountains and compare them to the Arctic.

2 Design an animal that could live in the Scottish mountains in winter. Draw the animal and describe its body covering, how it avoids predation and the changes that take place in winter.

Wordbank

Camouflage – hidden by colouring

Ermine – a stoat in winter colouring

Biodiversity is a shortened form of two words – biological diversity. The Earth's biodiversity describes all the living things that can survive the range of conditions that are currently found on this planet.

Species diversity

Species diversity includes all the kinds of living things on the planet. We are discovering new species of animals and plants all the time.

Figure 1 There is a huge range of living things

Biodiversity

Genetic diversity

Genetic diversity includes all the **genes** within one species – think about the different types of dogs or cats that you have seen.

Figure 2 This Great Dane and Yorkshire Terrier are both species of dog. There is a lot of genetic variation within some species

Genetic diversity supplies us with disease-resistant and high-yielding crops.

Ecological diversity

Ecological diversity refers to the variety of different habitats that exist on the planet.

Figure 3 A number of different habitats in Scotland

Ecological diversity gives us a range of habitats that ensure that the cycle of life is maintained to give us clean water and enough oxygen.

Today's problem

When the environment changes, living things can either evolve or become extinct.

Some people say: *"So what! Small numbers of living things cannot be very important anyway."* However scientists are becoming more and more concerned over the rapid decline of the earth's biodiversity.

Whenever a plant is lost, the habitat changes, all the animals that depend on that plant are affected and are at risk of **extinction** as well.

Extinction is a natural process, but biologists estimate that human activities have increased the rate of extinction on earth one hundred times or more. Species, genetic and ecological diversity are all under threat.

Figure 4 These human activities are causing reductions in biodiversity

Wordbank

Biodiversity – All the kinds of living things that are found on Earth (short for biological diversity)

Gene – The unit of inheritance, passed on from parents (e.g. eye colour in humans, size of dog or coat length in cats)

Extinction – Death of last member of a species

MSP – Member of Scottish parliament

Key ideas

★ Biodiversity refers to the diversity of species, genes and habitats

★ Biodiversity is being attacked by man's activities

★ Extinction of species is happening 100 times faster than it would naturally

Questions

1 Note two advantages from each of the three aspects of biodiversity.

2 Choose one aspect of biodiversity and write a letter to your **MSP** to protest at the extinction of living things.

One cold day Tina was sitting in class looking at the boys and girls in the playground.

She could see clouds coming from the mouths of the people in the playground. Most people seemed to be giving out small clouds but the pupils playing on the pitches seemed to be giving out more than those standing in the playground. She mentioned this to her friend Andrew, and he said that it has something to do with the fact that they were running about.

Figure 1 Breath condensing on cold days

Who do you think is correct?

You can investigate which pupil is correct.

Figure 2

The investigation

To plan the investigation properly you will have to:

1 State what you want to find out.

2 The equipment you will need.

3 The way the investigation will be done.

4 What you will measure to find out.

Fair testing

In order to get good results the investigation has to be done fairly.

This is what Tina and Andrew did.

- They took their chair to the front of the class and got a stopclock and a notebook.

- Tina sat on her chair and counted how many times she breathed in one minute. Andrew wrote this in the notebook.

- She then ran round the playground for two minutes and came back into the classroom.

- She sat down on the chair and counted how many times she breathed in the next minute. Andrew wrote this in his notebook.

Figure 3

Collecting Evidence

In an investigation it is important to get accurate results of the tests you do.

To try and make sure that what they were doing was scientific, Tina and Andrew did the same experiment again. This time Andrew counted his breaths and then ran round the playground, whilst Tina wrote in the notebook.

They put their results in a table like this:

Pupil	Number of breaths in one minute	
	Before exercise	After exercise
Tina	11	23
Andrew	12	26

They thought their results were quite interesting but felt that they would need to do more experiments to be sure that their investigation was correct.

The rest of the people in their group did the same as Tina and Andrew. They got the following results:

Pupil	Number of breaths in one minute	
	Before exercise	After exercise
Carol	13	29
Gordon	10	26
Iain	9	24
Hasan	10	30
Helen	14	25

Tina thought it would be a good idea to put their results on a bar chart (see Figure 4).

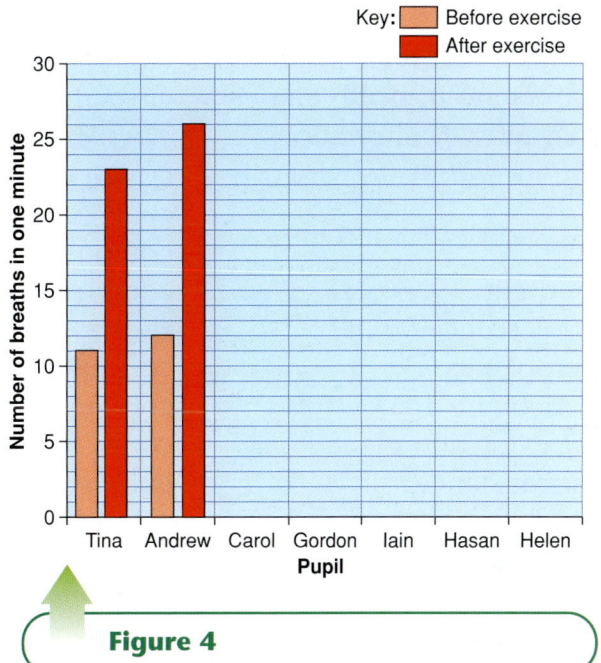

Key: Before exercise / After exercise

Figure 4

Questions

1 Why would Tina and Andrew feel happier by getting more people to do the experiment?

2 Should everyone do the same exercise round the playground?

3 What other factors could have an effect on their results?

4 Copy and complete the diagram for the other people in the group.

Further investigations

- You can investigate what other factors may cause your breathing to increase.

- Would the amount of exercise you do have an effect?

- If your breathing rate is high, what may help it to go down?

- Does exercise effect everyone's breathing by the same amount?

Index

(entries that refer to key words are in **bold**, entries that refer to illustrations are in *italics*)